The Torts Process

1992 Supplement

The Torts Process

Third Edition
1992 Supplement

James A. Henderson, Jr.

Frank B. Ingersoll Professor of Law
Cornell University Law School

Richard N. Pearson

Professor of Law
University of Florida College of Law

Little, Brown and Company
Boston   Toronto   London

Library of Congress Catalog Card No. 87-82335

ISBN 0-316-35646-8

Third Edition

EB

Published simultaneously in Canada
by Little, Brown & Company (Canada) Limited

Printed in the United States of America

Table of Contents

Table of Cases

Acknowledgments

This book supplements the third edition, and to thank all those who over the years have made significant contributions would make these pages unduly long. But some major contributors to this supplement deserve mention. Jylanda Diles, at Cornell University, took on the task of assembling and typing the manuscript; we could not have completed the task without her. We also would like to thank the student research assistants at Cornell Law School for their work on this supplement: David Bray, Jeff Roelofs, and Terry Toavs. Both law schools have provided all the assistance and encouragement we could wish for. We thank Deans Russell K. Osgood at Cornell and Jeffrey E. Lewis at Florida for that help.

We also thank the authors and publishers of the following for permitting us to include excerpts from these works:

J. Henderson and T. Eisenberg, The Quiet Revolution in Products Liability: An Empirical Study of Legal Change, 37 UCLA L. Rev. 479, 491 (1990). Reprinted by permission.

J. Henderson and A. Twerski, A Proposed Revision of Section 402A of the Restatement (Second) of Torts, 77 Cornell L. Rev. — (1992). Reprinted with the permission of the Cornell Law Review.

National Conference of Commissioners on Uniform State Laws, excerpt from the Model Uniform Employment Termination Act. Reprinted by permission.

National Conference of Commissioners on Uniform State Laws, excerpt from the discussion draft of the Uniform Defamation Act. Reprinted by permission.

The Torts Process

1992 Supplement

Part I

Introduction to the Process of
Resolving Torts Disputes

Chapter 1

The Intentional Infliction of Bodily Harm—Battery

B. The Substantive Law Governing Liability for Harmful Battery

2. Privileges

a. Consent

Page 51. Before Problem 3, add the following case:

Fricke v. Owens-Corning Fiberglas
571 So. 2d 130 (La. 1990)

DENNIS, Justice. In these actions, the plaintiffs seek to recover damages for intentional torts as the result of the death of one employee and the brain damage of a second which allegedly occurred when an employer's plant superintendent knowingly exposed the employees to the inhalation of toxic mustard vapors. The trial court granted defendants' motion for summary judgment, but the court of appeal reversed. Fricke v. Owens-Corning Fiberglas, 559 So. 2d 24 (La. App. 4th Cir. 1990). We reverse the court of appeal's judgment.

George Fricke, III, the 30 year old foreman of the mustard mill unit at Baumer Foods, Inc., looked down into an 18 foot deep mustard tank and saw Melvin Davillier, Sr. a fellow employee, lying unconscious at the bottom. He immediately fetched Roger Baumer, the 76 year old plant superintendent. Baumer started to descend a rope ladder inside the tank to rescue Davillier, but Fricke persuaded the older man to let him go instead. Baumer testified at his deposition as follows:

> Q: Going back up to the point in time when you and George [Fricke] arrived at the top of the catwalk and you looked into the tank and you saw Melvin [Davillier]—
>
> A: Right.

> *Q:* Just tell me what happened next without going into the whole story.
> I'd like to try to break it down into question and answer.
>
> *A:* I said I'll go down and get him [Davillier]. So I stepped over into the
> tank. I had one foot down on the ladder, and George said wait a
> minute. In other words, I looked like I was taking too long to get in
> there. George said I'm lighter than you. Let me go. And I said well,
> I'll go get a rope to pull him up.

Baumer's testimony is undisputed in the record presented for our review.

During Fricke's descent Baumer went for a rope and other employees to assist in the rescue. When they returned Fricke was prostrate at the bottom of the tank beside Davillier. A rescue unit of the fire department was summoned. Baumer employees and the firemen forced an opening in the tank wall and removed the men. Tragically, however, Davillier had suffered injuries which would later prove to be fatal and Fricke had sustained severe brain damage. Several actions ensued. . . .

The . . . defendants moved for summary judgment on the ground that these tort actions were barred by the exclusive remedy rule of the worker's compensation statute because there is no genuine issue as to the material facts; and that these facts reflect clearly that the accidental death and injury were due, at most, to the negligence of the superintendent rather than to his intentional act or tort. The trial court granted summary judgment terminating each action without assigning reasons. The plaintiffs appealed, and the court of appeal reversed. With respect to Fricke's injury the court concluded that a genuine issue of material fact exists as to whether Baumer's alleged act or omission in allowing Fricke to enter the tank to rescue Davillier was an intentional act or tort; therefore, summary judgment was improper. The court also reversed the trial court's summary judgment dismissing the Davillier action but failed to assign any reasons for its decision.

In this court the plaintiffs argue that Baumer's acts and omissions causing Fricke to go down into the mustard tank amounted to an intentional tort because: (a) Baumer desired to cause Fricke to come into harmful or offensive contact with the vapors in the mustard tank or believed that these consequences were substantially certain to result; and, (b) Baumer and his employer therefore are subject to liability for battery or other intentional tort because he acted intending to cause a harmful or offensive contact with Fricke's person and a harmful contact resulted. See Restatement (Second) of Torts, American Law Institute §§8A & 13 (1965). Plaintiffs correctly note that in order for Baumer to be liable it is not necessary that he intend to inflict actual damage or that his intention be malicious. It is sufficient if the actor intends to inflict either a harmful or offensive contact without the other's consent. Moreover, they aptly

4

observe that when a battery has been proved, the defendant's liability for the resulting harm extends, as in most other cases of intentional torts, to consequences which the defendant did not intend, and could not reasonably have foreseen, upon the obvious basis that it is better for unexpected losses to fall upon the intentional wrongdoer than upon the innocent victim.

All intended wrongs, however, have in common the element that they are inflicted without the consent of the victim. Consent therefore ordinarily bars recovery for intentional interferences with person or property. It is a fundamental principle of the common law that volenti non fit injuria—to one who is willing, no wrong is done. . . .

From our review of the summary judgment proceeding evidence, we conclude that there is no genuine dispute of material fact and that the defendants are entitled to judgment as a matter of law. In our opinion, based on the record presented, reasonable minds must inevitably conclude that Fricke consented to whatever offensive or harmful contact that Baumer desired or believed to a substantial certainty would befall Fricke when he descended to rescue Davillier. It is uncontroverted that neither Fricke nor Baumer knew that the mustard tank contained lethal or gravely damaging vapors; and that neither knew what had felled Davillier at the bottom. The evidence indicates without dispute that, although there had been some indication that the vapors had caused breathing difficulties to a few employees, in approximately 57 years of operations prior to the accident no employee had been rendered unconscious or seriously injured by the mustard tank's vapors.[20a]

For the reasons assigned, the judgment of the court of appeal is reversed and the judgments of the trial court are reinstated.

Reversed; summary judgments reinstated and affirmed.

20a. Of course, if Fricke in consenting to contact with the offensive vapors had been induced to do so by a substantial mistake as to the nature of the vapor or the extent of harm to be expected from it and the mistake had been known to Baumer or induced by Baumer's misrepresentation, Fricke's consent would not have been effective for the unexpected invasion or harm. See Restatement (Second) of Torts, American Law Institute §892B (1965). However, there is nothing to indicate that Baumer had any greater knowledge of the danger than Fricke or that Baumer knew of or induced Fricke's mistake. In fact, the record is convincing beyond any reasonable doubt that both Fricke and Baumer reacted as normal, decent human beings faced with the unprecedented distress of a fellow worker in an unforeseen emergency.

Part II

The Important Threshold Issues:
Identification of the Proper
Defendant and Evaluation of
the Plaintiff's Harm

Chapter 2

Cause-in-Fact

***Page 138.   After the last full paragraph, add
the following text and case:***

No area of products litigation in recent years captures the essence of
cause-in-fact analysis better than cases involving the widely used prescription drug Bendectin. Approved in 1956 by the Food and Drug Administration as a safe treatment for morning sickness during pregnancy,
Bendectin had been used by more than 30 million women between 1957
and 1983, when Richardson-Merrell, Inc., the manufacturer, withdrew it
from the market. Merrell withdrew the drug because of fears that it
caused severe birth defects in children of mothers who ingested the drug
while pregnant. A large number of tort claims had been filed based on
scientific studies, including epidemiological studies, allegedly revealing
the drug to be a teratogen, or birth-defect-causing agent. By the mid
1980s, Bendectin litigation appeared to be a growing area for plaintiffs'
lawyers. See, e.g., Oxendine v. Merrell Dow Pharmaceuticals, 506 A.2d
1100 (D.C. 1986) (Bendectin manufacturer held liable based on epidemiological proof of causation), *cert. denied,* 110 S. Ct. 1121 (1990).

Notwithstanding the optimism that reigned in the early to mid 1980s
among plaintiffs regarding the future of Bendectin litigation, the tide
began turning against them as the established scientific community concluded in a number of research projects that the link between the drug
and the birth defects had not been established at an adequate level of
statistical significance—that is, observed correlations between ingestion
and injury could have been the product of random chance. Courts hearing
these cases began to issue summary judgments for the defendant, Merrell,
with increasing frequency. A good example is Richardson v. Richardson-
Merrell, Inc., 857 F.2d 823 (D.C. Cir. 1988), *cert. denied,* 110 S. Ct. 218
(1989), in which the court of appeals affirmed a JNOV on behalf of
defendant, holding that, given the great weight of scientific opinion to
the contrary, plaintiff's expert's testimony on causation was insufficient.
The court concluded (857 F.2d at 832):

> The circumstances of the case are tragic and Carita Richardson's plight
> evokes the utmost sympathy. It would be foolhardy to expect members of

the jury to be without compassion for the catastrophe that befell this family. That is a natural response of the human spirit, and is without legal consequence so long as it is properly controlled. But in a case such as this it not only is appropriate but indeed imperative that the court remain vigilant to ensure that neither emotion nor confusion has supplanted reason. . . .

So certain was one of this book's authors that the Bendectin cases were over and done with that he made the following observations in an article published in 1990 (Henderson & Eisenberg, The Quiet Revolution in Products Liability: An Empirical Study of Legal Change, 37 UCLA L. Rev. 479, 491 (1990)):

A related area of products liability in which courts earlier appeared on the brink of a major, pro-plaintiff breakthrough involved manufacturers' liability for harm allegedly caused by Bendectin, a widely used morning sickness prescription remedy. These cases are significant because the only proof that the drug caused serious side effects in the newborn children of pregnant women who ingested the drug is epidemiologic. Experts can only say that the side effects appear to occur more frequently in the offspring of those who have taken the drug. Given the sympathetic reactions of several courts earlier in this decade to plaintiffs' epidemiologic proof of causation, one might have expected that Bendectin cases would be the next breakthrough for plaintiffs in the late 1980s and early 1990s. Several contrary decisions just last year, however, by influential federal courts of appeal, now make it unlikely that Bendectin-related claims have a promising future.[2a]

Consider the following decision, issued after the foregoing brave words of prediction.

DeLuca v. Merrell Dow Pharmaceuticals, Inc.
911 F.2d 941 (3d Cir. 1990)

STAPLETON, C.J.: This is an appeal in a diversity action brought under New Jersey law by the DeLuca family against Merrell Dow Pharmaceuticals Corporation, the manufacturer of Bendectin. The DeLucas seek damages for severe birth defects suffered by Cindy DeLuca's daughter Amy. Amy was born with limb reduction defects of the lower extremities:

2a. See, e.g., Brock v. Merrell Dow Pharmaceuticals, Inc., 874 F.2d 307, *modified on reh'g*, 884 F.2d 166 (5th Cir. 1989); Richardson v. Richardson-Merrell, Inc., 857 F.2d 823 (D.C. Cir. 1988), *cert. denied*, 110 S Ct. 218 (1989). The *Brock* opinion explicitly talks of "retreating" from the earlier, more generous approaches to plaintiff's epidemiological proof in cases of this sort. *Brock,* 874 F.2d at 311.

the lower portion of her left leg is deformed with anterior bowing of the tibia, absence of the fibula and three toes, and considerable shortening; and her right foot is missing a toe. The DeLucas allege that these birth defects were caused by Cindy DeLuca's use of Bendectin during the time she was pregnant with Amy.

Merrell Dow filed a motion for summary judgment alleging that the only causation evidence produced by the DeLucas was inadmissible because all relevant epidemiological studies have determined there is no statistically significant link between the use of Bendectin during pregnancy and the type of birth defects suffered by Amy DeLuca and these studies were the only reasonable basis for expert opinions. In response, the DeLucas proffered affidavits and deposition testimony by Dr. Alan Done, an expert in pediatric pharmacology, in which Dr. Done opined that the available epidemiological data does support the conclusion that Bendectin causes limb reduction defects and that he believed, to a reasonable degree of medical certainty, Bendectin caused Amy's defects. The district court held that Dr. Done's testimony would be inadmissible at trial because it was not based on data of a type reasonably relied upon by experts in the pertinent fields in issuing opinions on these subjects, as is required by Federal Rule of Evidence 703. Since Dr. Done's testimony was the sole causation evidence the DeLucas tendered in response to Merrell Dow's motion, the district court entered summary judgment for Merrell Dow. On appeal, the DeLucas argue that the district court misapplied Federal Rule of Evidence 703 in excluding Dr. Done's testimony. We agree and we will reverse and remand for proceedings consistent with the principles articulated herein.

I. The Legal and Scientific Setting

[The court's description of the factual background tracks that in the text preceding this case and is not reproduced.]

B. The Relevant Scientific Principles and Tendered Evidence

To competently analyze the legal issues presented by this appeal, an understanding of the relevant scientific principles, albeit necessarily a rudimentary one drawn primarily from the relevant sources cited to by the parties, is essential. Problematic issues of causation arise in Bendectin cases because the etiology of most birth defects is unknown. There is no apparent way to determine from clinical examinations of Amy DeLuca whether her limb defects were the result of her mother's exposure to Bendectin, as opposed to another possible teratogen, or whether her birth defects are simply an inexplicable natural occurrence not induced by her mother's exposure to an outside agent. Rather, the only particularistic evidence the DeLucas can show to strengthen the inference that Amy DeLuca's birth defects were caused by Bendectin is to rule in Bendectin as a possible cause by showing that Amy was exposed to it during the time her limbs were developing, i.e., during organogenesis, and to rule out other possible causes by showing that Amy was not exposed to them during the critical period of organogenesis. Merrell Dow did not contend before the district court that the DeLucas failed to present sufficient evidence in this regard.

Thus, the DeLucas must rely primarily on inferences drawn from epidemiological data to show causation in Amy's case. Epidemiology, a branch of science and medicine, uses studies to "observe the effect of exposure to a single factor upon the incidence of disease in two otherwise identical populations." Black & Lilienfeld, Epidemiological Proof In Toxic Tort Litigation, 52 Fordham L. Rev. 732, 755 (1984). In the Bendectin context, an epidemiological study ideally attempts to determine the incidence of birth defects among the children of two groups of women, identical in all respects except for their use of Bendectin during pregnancy. Epidemiological studies do not provide direct evidence that a particular plaintiff was injured by exposure to a substance. Such studies have the potential, however, of generating circumstantial evidence of cause and effect through a process known as hypothesis testing, a process which "amounts to an attempt to falsify the null hypothesis and by exclusion accept the alternative." K. J. Rothman, Modern Epidemiology 116 (1986) ("Rothman"). The null hypothesis is the hypothesis that there is no association between two studied variables, id.; in this case the key null hypothesis would be that there is no association between Bendectin exposure and an increase in limb reduction defects. The important alternative hypothesis in this case is that Bendectin use is associated with an increased incidence of limb reduction defects.

The great weight of scientific opinion, as is evidenced by . . . FDA committee results, sides with the view that Bendectin use does not increase the risk of having a child with birth defects. Sailing against the prevailing scientific breeze is the DeLucas' expert Dr. Alan Done, formerly a Professor of Pharmacology and Pediatrics at Wayne State University School of Medicine, who continues to hold fast to his position that Bendectin is a teratogen. In spite of his impressive curriculum vitae, Dr. Done's opinion on this subject has been rejected as inadmissible by several courts.

Dr. Done's opinion that Bendectin is a teratogen largely rests on inferences he draws from epidemiological data, most of which he contends are the same that [were] utilized by the experts, including the FDA committee, to whom Merrell Dow cites to bolster its contention that Bendectin does not cause birth defects. The principal difference is that Dr. Done analyzes that data using an approach, advocated by Professor Kenneth Rothman of the University of Massachusetts Medical School, that places diminished weight on so-called "significance testing." See K. J. Rothman, Modern Epidemiology (1986) ("Rothman"); see also, Rothman, A Show of Confidence, New Eng. J. of Medicine, Dec. 14, 1978, [at] 1362.

Epidemiological studies, of necessity, look to the experience of sample groups as indicative of the experience of a far larger population. Epidemiologists recognize, however, that the experience of the sample groups may vary from that of the larger population by chance. Thus, a showing of increased risk for birth defects among women using Bendectin in a particular study does not automatically prove that Bendectin use creates a higher risk of having a child with birth defects because the discrepancy between the exposed and unexposed groups could be the product of chance resulting from the use of only a small sample of the relevant populations. As a result of the acknowledged risk of this so-called "sampling error," researchers typically have rejected the associations suggested by epidemiological data unless those associations survive the rigors of "significance testing." This practice has also found favor in the legal context. A number of judicial opinions . . . have found Bendectin plaintiffs' causation evidence inadmissible because every published epidemiological study of the relationship of Bendectin exposure to the incidence of birth defects has concluded that there is not a "statistically significant" relationship between these two events.

Significance testing has a "P value" focus; the P value "indicates the probability, assuming the null hypothesis is true, that the observed data will depart from the absence of association to the extent that they actually do, or to a greater extent, by actual chance." Rothman, supra, at 116. If P is less than .05 (or 5%) a study's finding of a relationship supportive of the alternative hypothesis is considered statistically significant, if P is greater than 5% the relationship is rejected as insignificant. Accordingly, the results of a particular study are reported as simply "significant" or "not significant" or as $P > .05$ or $P < .05$.

Use of a .05 P value to determine whether to accept or reject the null hypothesis necessarily enhances one of two types of possible error. Type one error is when the null hypothesis is rejected when it is in fact true. Type two error is when the null hypothesis is in fact false but is not rejected. Rothman notes that at .05, the null hypothesis will "be rejected about 5 percent of the time when it is true," a relatively small risk of type one error. Id. at 117. Unfortunately, the relationship between type one error and type two error is not simple; however, one study in the context of an employment discrimination case concluded that when the risk of type one error equalled 5%, the risk of type two error was 50%. Cohen, Confidence in Probability: Burdens of Persuasion in a World of Imperfect Knowledge, 60 N.Y.U. L. Rev. 329, 411 & n.116 (1985) (citing Dawson, Investigation of Fact—The Role of the Statistician, 11 Forum 896, 907-08 (1976)). Type one error may be viewed here as the risk of concluding that Bendectin is a teratogen when it is not. Type two error is the risk of concluding that Bendectin is not a teratogen, when it in fact is.

Rothman contends that there is nothing magical or inherently important about .05 significance; rather this is just a common value on the tables scholars use to calculate significance. Rothman, supra, at 117; see also Cohen, supra, at 412 (noting that the .05 level of significance used in the social and physical sciences is a conservative and arbitrary value choice not necessarily valuable in the legal setting); Kaye, Is Proof of Statistical Significance Relevant?, 61 Wash. L. Rev. 1333, 1343-44 (1986). He stresses that the data in a certain study may indicate a strong relationship between two variables but still not be "statistically significant" and that the level of significance which should be required depends on the type of decision being made and the relative values placed on avoiding the two types of risk. . . .

C.   The Bendectin Case Law

We recognize that the district court's decision to exclude Dr. Done's proposed testimony was heavily influenced by the decisions of other courts that have grappled with the difficult question of whether expert testimony that Bendectin causes birth defects is admissible and/or sufficient to sustain a verdict. A review of these cases is thus helpful. . . .

[The court's description of previous cases, including the *Richardson* decision quoted in the text preceding this decision, is omitted.]

We understand and sympathize with the concerns expressed in [a previous case] over the costs and inequities that flow from inconsistent outcomes in Bendectin cases, the potential effect erroneous verdicts have on the availability of useful medicines, and the wastefulness of continued reconsideration of an identical scientific issue in the courts. We are also troubled . . . by the potential for abuse that exists whenever an expert is permitted to testify to an opinion that is based upon reasoning and data that have not been subjected to the review of professional colleagues. This concern is naturally heightened when an expert is testifying on behalf of a plaintiff as sympathetic as a child crippled by serious birth defects.

However, our concern over these issues is tempered by our recognition that we do not have the authority to create special rules to address the problems posed by continued Bendectin litigation. Principles of issue preclusion have not developed to the point where we may bind plaintiffs by the finding of previous proceedings in which they were not parties, even by a proceeding as thorough as the multidistrict common issues trial. . . . Moreover, we may not manipulate our interpretation of the Federal Rules of Evidence to exclude expert testimony that on the record before us may satisfy normal standards of admissibility. Nor are we at liberty, especially in a case to be decided under our diversity jurisdiction, to impose different burdens of proof on Bendectin plaintiffs than those that would apply in analogous products liability suits. At the same time, however, we must require that Bendectin plaintiffs carry the evidentiary burdens imposed upon other plaintiffs. That is, plaintiffs must produce admissible evidence from which a jury could, applying the requisite burden of proof, reasonably find that their injuries were caused by Bendectin.

On a typical summary judgment motion in a Bendectin case, a court's task is essentially two-fold: (1) to scrutinize the admissibility of the plaintiff's expert testimony under the Federal Rules of Evidence, and (2) to measure what is admissible against the appropriate state law standard governing causation to determine whether summary judgment is appropriate. We address these issues in turn.

II. The Admissibility Issues

A. Rule 703. . .

In the present case, the district court purported to apply the correct standard. However, its cursory ruling that Done's testimony was inadequate under Rule 703 does not comply with the standard set forth in [a previous decision] as it was not predicated upon a record-supported, factual finding that Done relied upon identified data not regarded as reliable by experts in the field. Instead, the analysis in the district court's opinion referred only to Dr. Done's qualifications and the case law we have previously discussed indicating that the testimony of Dr. Done, or similar testimony, is inadmissible under Rule 703.

The district court appeared to discard Dr. Done's reanalysis of the available epidemiological evidence in part because he is not an epidemiologist. This was improper given Merrell Dow's concession that Dr. Done was qualified to interpret epidemiological data. It was also erroneous because an objection to Dr. Done's qualifications should be analyzed under Rule of Evidence 702, not Rule 703. Given the liberal criteria that govern the expertness inquiry, . . . it is doubtful whether an expert with Dr. Done's credentials could be precluded from testifying about his interpretation of epidemiological evidence simply because he does not have a degree in epidemiology.

Putting aside the substantial question of whether the records in the prior Bendectin cases were materially different from the record here, these prior judicial opinions cannot sustain the district court's ruling because they do not address the question of whether reasonable experts would rely upon the epidemiological data Dr. Done bases his opinion on; rather, they primarily turn on the failure of that data to show a "statistically significant" link between Bendectin and an increased incidence of birth defects, and on the weight of scientific opinion contrary to Dr. Done's view that Bendectin is a teratogen.

While these factors may not be irrelevant to another type of challenge to Dr. Done's testimony, as we discuss hereafter, we do not view the absence of statistically significant findings or the great weight of contrary opinion as being relevant to the Rule 703 question posed here. Rule 703 is satisfied once there is a showing that an expert's testimony is based on the type of data a reasonable expert in the field would use in rendering an opinion on the subject at issue; it does not address the reliability or general acceptance of an expert's methodology. When a statistician refers to a study as "not statistically significant," he is not making a statement about the reliability of the data used, rather he is making a statement about the propriety of drawing a particular inference from that data.[2b]

At oral argument, counsel for Merrell Dow conceded that Merrell Dow had not specifically challenged the data Dr. Done relied upon. Indeed, with respect to most of Dr. Done's data, Merrell Dow is hardly in a position to claim that it is not of a type reasonably relied upon by experts in the field since Merrell Dow's expert relied upon the same epidemiological data from the published literature in formulating her opinion. To the extent Merrell Dow wishes to challenge particular sets of data Dr. Done has used, it is free to do so on remand. However, it has not attempted to show that Dr. Done's reliance upon particular epidemiological data is unreasonable, and the DeLucas had no burden to address arguments not made. . . .

2b. He is making a statement about the degree to which the relationship found in the data may be due to chance, but his decision to use a certain significance level as a check on the permissible inference to be drawn from the data is a methodological value judgment which is separate from the question of whether the data is of the type an expert would rely upon.

Implicit in the district court's decision . . . is the principle that Rule 703 requires an expert to accept the conclusions reached by the authors of studies if the expert wishes to utilize the data underlying those studies as a basis for testimony. However, the Federal Rules of Evidence contain no requirement that an expert's testimony be based upon reasoning subjected to peer-review and published in the professional literature. . . .

B.   Rule 702

While Merrell Dow has not challenged the reliability of specific data utilized by Dr. Done, it has challenged before us the way in which he has used his data on a number of grounds, each of which it is free to pursue on remand. As we have noted, Merrell Dow's principal emphasis in this regard has been its insistence that an expert opinion based on epidemiological data and analysis is not admissible unless the data "disprove" the null hypothesis that Bendectin is not a teratogen at a .05 level of "statistical significance." This argument presents an issue of first impression in this circuit. We conclude that it should be evaluated under Rule 702 and in accordance with the teachings of United States v. Downing, 753 F.2d 1224 (3d Cir. 1985).

Rule 702 provides:

> If scientific, technical or other specialized knowledge will assist the trier of fact to understand the evidence or to determine a fact in issue, a witness qualified as an expert by knowledge, skill, experience, training, or education, may testify thereto in the form of an opinion or otherwise.

Rule 702 authorizes the admission of expert testimony so long as it is rendered by a qualified expert and is helpful to the trier of fact. . . . While no Federal Rule of Evidence specifically addresses the methodological fundamentals for expert testimony, Rule 702's helpfulness requirement implicitly contains the proposition that expert testimony that is based on unreliable methodology is unhelpful and therefore excludable. *Downing*, 753 F.2d 1224.

The reliability of expert testimony founded on reasoning from epidemiological data is generally a fit subject for judicial notice; epidemiology is a well-established branch of science and medicine, and epidemiological evidence has been accepted in numerous cases. . . .

To the extent that the reliability of Dr. Done's mode of analysis is not susceptible of judicial notice, i.e., deviates from that which has consistently been admitted into evidence, however, the district court on remand must conduct a hearing and analysis consistent with the counsel provided in *Downing*. In that case this court articulated a flexible test for addressing contentions that expert testimony based on arguably unreliable techniques were "unhelpful" and thus inadmissible under Rule 702:

> Rule 702 requires that a district court ruling upon the admission of (novel) scientific evidence, i.e. evidence whose scientific fundaments are not suitable candidates for judicial notice, conduct a preliminary inquiry focusing on (1) the soundness and reliability of the process or technique used in generating the evidence, (2) the possibility that admitting the evidence would overwhelm, confuse, or mislead the jury, and (3) the proffered connection between the scientific research or test result to be presented, and particular disputed factual issues in the case.

Id. at 1237.[2c] The "fit" between Dr. Done's tendered testimony and the crucial causation issues in this case is a good one and the third *Downing* factor thus cuts in favor of its admissibility. It is the other factors, reliability and jury reaction, that the district court will need to address if Merrell Dow litigates this issue on remand. . . .

By directing such an overall evaluation, however, we do not mean to reject at this point Merrell Dow's contention that a showing of a .05 level of statistical significance should be a threshold requirement for any statistical analysis concluding that Bendectin is a teratogen regardless of the presence of other indicia of reliability. That contention will need to be addressed on remand. The root issue it poses is what risk of what type of error the judicial system is willing to tolerate. This is not an easy issue to resolve and one possible resolution is a conclusion that the system should not tolerate any expert opinion rooted in statistical analysis where the results of the underlying studies are not significant at a .05 level. We believe strongly, however, that this issue should not be resolved in a case where the record contains virtually no relevant help from the parties or from qualified experts. The literature evidences that there are legal scholars and epidemiologists who have given considerable thought to this and

---

2c. While it is true that *Downing* can be read as applying only to so-called "novel" scientific evidence, see 753 F.2d at 1237, this is an unduly restricted reading of the opinion. The importance of *Downing* is in the framework it provides for analyzing claims that proffered scientific evidence is insufficiently trustworthy to be admissible. Where the "helpfulness" of expert testimony cannot be resolved via judicial notice, *Downing* sets forth the test for assessing the admissibility of the testimony.

related issues and we would hope that this expertise could be made available to the court, on remand, in some acceptable manner. . . .

After considering the reliability of Dr. Done's testimony and the dangers it poses, the district court will have to reach the ultimate determination of whether it is "helpful" and thus admissible. That determination will require an exercise of discretion informed by the teachings of *Downing* and the record developed on remand. Once made, it will be entitled to deference. . . .

III.   *The Sufficiency of the Evidence Issue*

Since the district court held that the DeLucas' sole evidence of causation was inadmissible, it had no difficulty in concluding that they had not met their burden under the Celotex trilogy to produce evidence sufficient to raise a genuine issue of material fact as to whether Amy DeLuca's birth defects were caused by Bendectin. . . . If Dr. Done's testimony is ultimately held to be admissible, however, a different issue will be presented. While we express no opinion on that issue, we wish to make clear that nothing in this opinion is intended to suggest that this issue is or is not susceptible of resolution by summary judgment.

. . . In the present context, Dr. Done's testimony may be found sufficiently helpful to be admissible and sufficiently probative to support a jury finding that Bendectin can cause birth defects or even that Bendectin not infrequently causes such defects. However, assuming that New Jersey would apply the traditional "more probable than not" burden of proof standard to the causation issue in this case, this admissible testimony would not alone bar summary judgment for Merrell Dow unless it would support a jury finding that Bendectin more likely than not caused the birth defects in this particular case.

Hypothetically, Dr. Done may be able to testify, on the basis of adequate data and the application of reasonably reliable methodology, for example, that of women who took Bendectin and had children with birth defects, 25% of the cases of birth defects can be attributed to Bendectin exposure. This testimony would be admissible as it would be a basis from which a jury could rationally find that Bendectin could have caused Amy DeLuca's birth defects; however, it would not without more suffice to satisfy the DeLucas' burden on causation under a more likely than not standard since a fact finder could not say on the basis of this evidence alone that Amy DeLuca's birth defects were more likely than not caused by Bendectin.

If New Jersey law requires the DeLucas to show that it is more likely than not that Bendectin caused Amy DeLuca's birth defects, and they are forced to rely solely on Dr. Done's epidemiological analysis in order to avoid summary judgment, the relative risk of limb reduction defects arising from the epidemiological data Done relies upon will, at a minimum, have to exceed "2":

> A relative risk of "2" means that the disease occurs among the population subject to the event under investigation twice as frequently as the disease occurs among the population not subject to the event under investigation. Phrased another way, a relative risk of "2" means that, on the average, there is a fifty per cent likelihood that a particular case of the disease was caused by the event under investigation and a fifty per cent likelihood that the disease was caused by chance alone. A relative risk greater than "2" means that the disease more likely than not was caused by the event.

Manko v. United States, 636 F. Supp. 1419, 1434 (W.D. Mo. 1986), aff'd in relevant part, 830 F.2d 831 (8th Cir. 1987).

We express no opinion on whether Dr. Done's epidemiological analysis fails to meet this threshold requirement. While it is not clear to our untrained eyes that it does, without the benefit of an expert affidavit critiquing that analysis we are not sufficiently confident of our own critical capacities to resolve that issue. Nor do we suggest that the DeLucas will be required to rely solely on Dr. Done's epidemiological analysis at trial or in any subsequent summary judgment proceedings. The alternative support that he finds for his conclusion in structural activity analysis, for example, may be entitled to some weight in determining whether they have met their burden of establishing a prima facie case. We note only that even if Dr. Done's epidemiological analysis is found to be admissible, the DeLucas are entitled to get to trial only if the district court is satisfied that this analysis together with any other evidence relevant to the causation issue would permit a jury finding that Amy's birth defects were, when measured against the appropriate burden of proof, caused by her mother's exposure to Bendectin.

IV. Conclusion

We hold that the present record cannot sustain the exclusion of Dr. Done's testimony. Therefore, we will reverse the grant of summary judgment in Merrell Dow's favor and remand for further proceedings consistent with this opinion.

Page 139.   *After the carryover paragraph, add the following new case:*

Falcon v. Memorial Hospital
436 Mich. 443, 462 N.W.2d 44 (1990)

LEVIN, Justice

IV

Nena Falcon, a nineteen-year-old woman, gave birth to a healthy baby. . . . Moments after delivery, Nena Falcon coughed, gagged, convulsed, became cyanotic, and suffered a complete respiratory and cardiac collapse. Attempts to revive her were unsuccessful. She was pronounced dead soon thereafter.

The autopsy report indicated that amniotic fluid embolism, an unpreventable complication that occurs in approximately one out of ten or twenty thousand births, was the cause of death. The survival rate of amniotic fluid embolism is, according to Falcon's expert witness, 37.5 percent if an intravenous line is connected to the patient before the onset of embolism. In this case, an intravenous line had not been established.

Falcon's theory is that had a physician or nurse anesthetist inserted an intravenous line before administering the spinal anesthetic to assist the physician in dealing with any of several complications, the intravenous line could have been used to infuse live-saving fluids into Nena Falcon's circulatory system, providing her a 37.5 percent opportunity of surviving. By not inserting the intravenous line, the physician deprived her of a 37.5 percent opportunity of surviving the embolism.

V

The question whether a defendant caused an event is not readily answered, and is especially perplexing in circumstances such as those present in the instant case where the defendant's failure to act is largely responsible for the uncertainty regarding causation.

Had the defendants in the instant case inserted an intravenous line, one of two things would have happened, Nena Falcon would have lived, or she would have died. There would be no uncertainty whether the omissions of the defendants caused her death. Falcon's destiny would have been decided by fate and not possibly by her health care providers. . . .

VI

In an ordinary tort action seeking recovery for physical harm, the defendant is a stranger to the plaintiff and the duty imposed by operation of law is imposed independently of any undertaking by the defendant. In an action claiming medical malpractice, however, the patient generally is not a stranger to the defendant. Generally, the patient engaged the services of the defendant physician. The physician undertook to perform services for the patient, and the patient undertook to pay or provide payment for the services.

The scope of the undertakings by a physician or hospital to the patient and by the patient to the physician or hospital is not generally a matter of express agreement. There is, however, an understanding that the law enforces in the absence of express agreement. The patient expects a physician to do that which is expected of physicians of like training in the community, and the physician expects the patient to pay or provide payment for the services, whether the likelihood of there in fact being any benefit to the patient is only one through fifty percent or is greater than fifty percent.

The defendants assert, in effect, that the scope of their undertaking did not include acts or omissions likely to benefit the patient only to the extent of one through fifty percent—or at least they should not be subject to liability for acts or omissions likely to have caused harm to the extent only of one through fifty percent. They contend that they should be subject to liability only for acts or omissions likely, to the extent of more than fifty percent, to have caused physical harm to the patient. . . .

Patients engage the services of doctors, not only to prevent disease or death, but also to delay death and to defer or ameliorate the suffering associated with disease or death. If the trier of fact were to decide, on the basis of expert testimony, that the undertaking of the defendant physician included the implementation of tasks and procedures that, in the case of Nena Falcon, would have enabled the physician and other medically trained persons, who were present at the time of delivery, to provide her, in the event of the medical accident that occurred, an opportunity to survive the accident, a failure to do so was a breach of the understanding or undertaking.

Nena Falcon, if the testimony of Falcon's expert witness is credited, would have had a 37.5 percent opportunity of surviving had the defendants implemented the procedures Falcon's expert asserts should have been implemented. In reducing Nena Falcon's opportunity of living by failing to insert an intravenous line, her physician caused her harm, although it cannot be said, more probably than not, that he caused her death. A

37.5 percent opportunity of living is hardly the kind of opportunity that any of us would willingly allow our health care providers to ignore. If, as Falcon's expert asserts, the implementation of such procedures was part of the understanding or undertaking, the failure to have implemented the procedures was a breach of the understanding or undertaking. The physician is, and should be, subject to liability for such breach, although Nena Falcon was likely, measured as more than fifty percent, to die as soon as the medical accident occurred and the negligence of the physician eliminated a less than fifty percent opportunity of surviving.

We thus see the injury resulting from medical malpractice as not only, or necessarily, physical harm, but also as including the loss of opportunity of avoiding physical harm. A patient goes to a physician precisely to improve his opportunities of avoiding, ameliorating, or reducing physical harm and pain and suffering.

Women gave birth to children long before there were physicians or hospitals or even midwives. A woman who engages the services of a physician and enters a hospital to have a child does so to reduce pain and suffering and to increase the likelihood of her surviving and the child surviving childbirth in a good state of health even though the likelihood of the woman and child not surviving in good health without such services is far less than fifty percent. That is why women go to physicians. That is what physicians undertake to do. That is what they are paid for. They are, and should be, subject to liability if they fail to measure up to the standard of care.

VII

A number of courts have recognized, as we would, loss of an opportunity for a more favorable result, as distinguished from the unfavorable result, as compensable in medical malpractice actions. Under this approach, damages are recoverable for the loss of opportunity although the opportunity lost was less than even, and thus it is not more probable than not that the unfavorable result would or could have been avoided. . . .

VIII . . .

We are persuaded that loss of a 37.5 percent opportunity of living constitutes a loss of a substantial opportunity of avoiding physical harm. We need not now decide what lesser percentage would constitute a substantial loss of opportunity.

IX

In the instant case, while Nena Falcon's cause of action accrued before her death, she did not suffer conscious pain and suffering from the failure to implement the omitted procedures between the moment that the medical accident occurred and the time of her death a few minutes later— she was sedated throughout the entire time period. In this case, 37.5 percent times the damages recoverable for wrongful death would be an appropriate measure of damages.

We would affirm the Court of Appeals reversal of the entry of summary judgment for the defendants, and remand the case for trial.

[The concurring opinion of BOYLE, J., and the dissenting opinion of RILEY, C.J., are omitted.]

Chapter 4

Damages

A. Compensatory Damages

1. Personal Injury

b. Lost Earnings and Impairment of Earning Capacity

(1)   The Basic Measure of Recovery

Page 218.   After **Healy v. White,** *insert the following new case:*

Mauro v. Raymark Industries, Inc.
116 N.J. 126, 561 A.2d 257 (1989)

STEIN, J. . . .

1.

Plaintiffs, Roger Mauro (hereinafter plaintiff) and Lois Mauro, his wife, instituted this action against several manufacturers of asbestos products based on injuries allegedly sustained as a result of inhalation of asbestos fibers in the course of Mauro's employment at Ancora State Psychiatric Hospital. . . .

In 1981 plaintiff and his co-workers participated in tests conducted by the New Jersey Department of Health to determine the prevalence of asbestos-related disease among plumbers and steamfitters in state institutions. Plaintiff was informed by Dr. Peter Gann, the department's Chief of Occupational Medicine, that although the results of his physical examination and lung function test were "normal," he had bilateral thickening of both chest walls and calcification of the diaphragm. Dr. Gann's letter informing plaintiff of his condition stated: "[Y]our exposure to asbestos has been significant and there is some evidence that this exposure may increase the risk of development of lung cancer."

Mauro testified that when informed of his condition, he became "very angry, very upset." He feared contracting cancer because his mother and a prior employer had died of the disease. He subsequently consulted a pulmonary specialist, by whom he has been examined every six months since 1982. Mauro has also had annual chest x-rays. He testified that the reason for his medical surveillance is "to find out if I'm going to get cancer and when I'm going to get it."

[Plaintiff's expert] Dr. Guidice . . . acknowledged that he did not testify that it was probable that Mauro would contract cancer: "There's a risk. . . . I certainly can't predict he's going to get cancer. All I can say is there's a high probability he's at risk because he's a young man and therefore he's at increased risk . . . for developing cancer."

In its charge to the jury at the conclusion of the trial, the trial court rejected Mauro's claim for enhanced risk of developing cancer. The court explained:

> There's no testimony that the Plaintiff Roger has cancer or that he likely will get cancer. In New Jersey damages may not be awarded for any future injury which is merely possible but not probable.
>
> The reason for this rule is simple. In this state, if the Plaintiff were to get cancer sometime in the future and claim same to have been due to an alleged asbestos exposure, at that point he could file a new lawsuit seeking damages for that cancer.
>
> Accordingly, even if you conclude that the plaintiff has an enhanced risk of developing cancer, you may not award any damages for that risk.

However, the court permitted the jury to consider Mauro's claim for damages caused by emotional distress relating to his fear of developing cancer, provided the jury found that Mauro sustained an asbestos-related injury. The court also permitted the jury to consider Mauro's claim for damages caused by his present medical condition, as well as the cost of future medical surveillance.

[The jury returned a verdict for the plaintiff Roger Mauro for $7,500. The judgment for the plaintiff on the jury verdict was affirmed by the Appellate Division.]

II. . . .

The long-standing rule in New Jersey is that prospective damages are not recoverable unless they are reasonably probable to occur. [The court's discussion of New Jersey cases, law review commentary, and cases from other states is omitted.]

Nor is there any question concerning the right of a plaintiff who has sustained physical injury because of exposure to toxic chemicals to recover damages for emotional distress based on a reasonable concern that he or she has an enhanced risk of further disease. . . . On appeal, defendants urged that the claim was not cognizable because of a lack of physical symptoms evidencing plaintiff's distress. . . . [A]lthough we need not and do not reach the question whether exposure to toxic chemicals without physical injury would sustain a claim for emotional distress damages based on a reasonable fear of future disease, such a damage claim is clearly cognizable where, as here, plaintiff's exposure to asbestos has resulted in physical injury. . . .

Although the weight of authority compellingly argues against recognition of an enhanced-risk-of-cancer claim by a plaintiff with an asbestos-related injury absent proof that satisfies the standard of reasonable medical probability, our analysis would be incomplete without consideration of policy arguments that oppose the general rule. Foremost among these is the concern that deferral of the prospective-injury claim may preclude any recovery when the disease eventually occurs because of the substantial difficulties inherent in attempting to prove causation in toxic-tort cases. If the enhanced-risk claim is deferred, a plaintiff asserting the claim when the second injury occurs will inevitably confront the defense that the injury did not result from exposure to toxic chemicals but was "the product of intervening events or causes."

Recognition of a claim for significantly enhanced risk of disease would also enhance the tort-law's capacity to deter the improper use of toxic chemicals and substances, thereby addressing the contention that tort law cannot deter polluters who view the cost of proper use or disposal as exceeding the risk of tort liability.

The rule of reasonable medical probability is also challenged as an artificial, all-or-nothing standard that rejects future-injury claims supported by substantial evidence that barely falls short of the required quantum of proof. . . .

Other considerations weigh in favor of limiting recognition of enhanced-risk claims to those that prove to a reasonable medical probability the likelihood of future injury. Those claims that fail to meet this standard, if presented to juries, would require damage awards for diseases that are prospective, speculative, and less than likely to occur. The more speculative the proof of future disease, the more difficult would be the juries' burden of calculating fair compensation. Inevitably, damage awards would be rendered for diseases that will never occur, exacting a societal cost in the form of higher insurance premiums and higher product costs.

The vast number of asbestos-related claims now pending in state and federal courts throughout the country is a matter of public record. The formidable burden of litigating such claims would be significantly greater if a substantial percentage of these cases also involved disposition of damage claims for the relatively unquantified enhanced risk of future disease.

Equally persuasive to this Court, however, is the availability of a future opportunity to assert such claims if and when the disease occurs, combined with the present availability of medical surveillance and emotional distress damages in appropriate cases. In our view, removal of the statute-of-limitations and single-controversy doctrines as a bar to the institution of suit when the disease for which plaintiff is at risk ultimately occurs enhances the quality of the remedy that tort law can provide in such cases. If the disease never occurs, presumably there will be no claim and no recovery. If it does occur, the resultant litigation will involve a tangible claim for present injury, rather than a speculative claim for future injury. Hence, juries will be better able to award damages in an amount that fairly reflects the nature and severity of the plaintiff's injury.

We acknowledge that our resolution of this issue is imperfect. In asbestos cases, for example, the available statistical evidence correlating asbestos-related disease with the future onset of cancer appears to fall short—as was evident from the evidence proffered in this case—of establishing the occurrence of cancer as a matter of reasonable medical probability. Undoubtedly, there will be individual cases in which statistical evidence, combined with the particular degree of exposure and injury sustained by the plaintiff, will establish the likelihood of future disease as a matter of probability. With respect to those cases in which the evidence that future disease will occur falls substantially short of the reasonable-medical-probability standard, we are satisfied that the interests of justice are well served by excluding such claims from jury consideration. Of course, there will be close cases, and for their resolution our use of the reasonable-medical-probability standard "to draw judicial lines beyond which liability will not be extended is fundamentally . . . an instrument of fairness and policy." Caputzal v. The Lindsay Co., 48 N.J. 69, 77, 222 A.2d 513 (1966). The standard of reasonable medical probability has been applied in New Jersey since at least 1957. See Budden v. Goldstein, 43 N.J. Super. at 347, 128 A.2d 730 [(1957)]. The rationale then advanced for the rule bears repetition here:

> [A] consequence of an injury which is possible, which may possibly ensue, is a risk which the injured person must bear because the law cannot be administered so as to do reasonably efficient justice if conjecture and speculation are to be used as a measure of damages. On the other hand, a consequence which stands on the plane of reasonable probability, although it is not certain to occur, may be considered in the evaluation of the damage claim against the defendant. In this way, to the extent that men can achieve justice through general rules, a just balance of the warring interests is accomplished. [Id.]

By adapting the statute-of-limitations and the single-controversy doctrines to the realities of toxic-tort cases, we have ameliorated the potential unfairness of applying the reasonable-probability standard to this type of litigation. Moreover, our case law affords toxic-tort plaintiffs the right to receive full compensation for any provable diminution of bodily health, accommodating all damage claims attributable to present injury and deferring compensation only for disease not yet incurred and not reasonably probable to occur. Recognition of present claims for medical surveillance and emotional distress realistically addresses significant aspects of the present injuries sustained by toxic-tort plaintiffs, and serves as an added deterrent to polluters and others responsible for the wrongful use of toxic chemicals. In our view, these developments in New Jersey law affecting toxic-tort plaintiffs argue persuasively against modification of the reasonable-probability standard in such cases. We therefore will not disturb the trial court's refusal to submit to the jury plaintiff's damage claim based on his enhanced risk of cancer. . . .

Judgment affirmed.

[The dissenting opinion of HANDLER, J., is omitted.]

c. Pain, Suffering, and Other Intangible Elements

Page 239. After Walters v. Hitchcock, add the following new case:

McDougald v. Garber
73 N.Y.2d 246, 536 N.E.2d 372 (1989)

WACHTLER, Chief Judge. This appeal raises fundamental questions about the nature and role of nonpecuniary damages in personal injury litigation. By nonpecuniary damages, we mean those damages awarded to compensate an injured person for the physical and emotional consequences of the injury, such as pain and suffering and the loss of the ability to engage in certain activities. Pecuniary damages, on the other hand, compensate the victim for the economic consequences of the injury, such as medical expenses, lost earnings and the cost of custodial care.

The specific questions raised here deal with assessment of nonpecuniary damages and are (1) whether some degree of cognitive awareness is a prerequisite to recovery for loss of enjoyment of life and (2) whether a jury should be instructed to consider and award damages for loss of enjoyment of life separately from damages for pain and suffering. We answer the first question in the affirmative and the second question in the negative.

I.

On September 7, 1978, plaintiff Emma McDougald, then 31 years old, underwent a Caesarean section and tubal ligation at New York Infirmary. Defendant Garber performed the surgery; defendants Armengol and Kulkarni provided anesthesia. During the surgery, Mrs. McDougald suffered oxygen deprivation which resulted in severe brain damage and left her in a permanent comatose condition. This action was brought by Mrs. McDougald and her husband, suing derivatively, alleging that the injuries were caused by the defendants' acts of malpractice.

A jury found all defendants liable and awarded Emma McDougald a total of $9,650,102 in damages, including $1,000,000 for conscious pain and suffering and a separate award of $3,500,000 for loss of the pleasures and pursuits of life. The balance of the damages awarded to her were for pecuniary damages—lost earnings and the cost of custodial and nursing care. Her husband was awarded $1,500,000 on his derivative claim for the loss of his wife's services. On defendants' posttrial motions, the Trial Judge reduced the total award to Emma McDougald to $4,796,728 by striking the entire award for future nursing care ($2,353,374) and by reducing the separate awards for conscious pain and suffering and loss of the pleasures and pursuits of life to a single award of $2,000,000 (McDougald v. Garber, 132 Misc. 2d 457, 504 N.Y.S.2d 383). Her husband's award was left intact. On cross appeals, the Appellate Division affirmed (135 A.D.2d 80, 524 N.Y.S.2d 192) and later granted defendants leave to appeal to this court.

II.

. . . At trial, defendants sought to show that Mrs. McDougald's injuries were so severe that she was incapable of either experiencing pain or appreciating her condition. Plaintiffs, on the other hand, introduced proof that Mrs. McDougald responded to certain stimuli to a sufficient extent to indicate that she was aware of her circumstances. Thus, the extent of Mrs. McDougald's cognitive abilities, if any, was sharply disputed.

The parties and the trial court agreed that Mrs. McDougald could not recover for pain and suffering unless she were conscious of the pain. Defendants maintained that such consciousness was also required to support an award for loss of enjoyment of life. The court, however, accepted plaintiffs' view that loss of enjoyment of life was compensable without regard to whether the plaintiff was aware of the loss. Accordingly, because the level of Mrs. McDougald's cognitive abilities was in dispute, the court instructed the jury to consider loss of enjoyment of life as an element of nonpecuniary damages separate from pain and suffering. . . .

We conclude that the court erred, both in instructing the jury that Mrs. McDougald's awareness was irrelevant to their consideration of damages for loss of enjoyment of life and in directing the jury to consider that aspect of damages separately from pain and suffering.

III.

We begin with the familiar proposition that an award of damages to a person injured by the negligence of another is to compensate the victim, not to punish the wrongdoer. The goal is to restore the injured party, to the extent possible, to the position that would have been occupied had the wrong not occurred. To be sure, placing the burden of compensation on the negligent party also serves as a deterrent, but purely punitive damages—that is, those which have no compensatory purpose—are prohibited unless the harmful conduct is intentional, malicious, outrageous, or otherwise aggravated beyond mere negligence.

Damages for nonpecuniary losses are, of course, among those that can be awarded as compensation to the victim. This aspect of damages, however, stands on less certain ground than does an award for pecuniary damages. An economic loss can be compensated in kind by an economic gain; but recovery for noneconomic losses such as pain and suffering and loss of enjoyment of life rests on "the legal fiction that money damages can compensate for a victim's injury" (Howard v. Lecher, 42 N.Y.2d 109, 111, 397 N.Y.S.2d 363, 366 N.E.2d 64). We accept this fiction, knowing that although money will neither ease the pain nor restore the victim's abilities, this device is as close as the law can come in its effort to right the wrong. We have no hope of evaluating what has been lost, but a monetary award may provide a measure of solace for the condition created.

Our willingness to indulge this fiction comes to an end, however, when it ceases to serve the compensatory goals of tort recovery. When that limit is met, further indulgence can only result in assessing damages that are punitive. The question posed by this case, then, is whether an award of damages for loss of enjoyment of life to a person whose injuries preclude any awareness of the loss serves a compensatory purpose. We conclude that it does not.

Simply put, an award of money damages in such circumstances has no meaning or utility to the injured person. An award for the loss of enjoyment of life "cannot provide [such a victim] with any consolation or ease any burden resting on him . . . He cannot spend it upon necessities or pleasures. He cannot experience the pleasure of giving it away" (Flannery v. United States, 4th Cir., 718 F.2d 108, 111, *cert. denied* 467 U.S. 1226, 104 S. Ct. 2679, 81 L. Ed. 2d 874).

We recognize that, as the trial court noted, requiring some cognitive awareness as a prerequisite to recovery for loss of enjoyment of life will result in some cases "in the paradoxical situation that the greater the degree of brain injury inflicted by a negligent defendant, the smaller the award the plaintiff can recover in general damages" (McDougald v. Garber, 132 Misc. 2d 457, 460, 504 N.Y.S.2d 383, supra). The force of this argument, however—the temptation to achieve a balance between injury and damages—has nothing to do with meaningful compensation for the victim. Instead, the temptation is rooted in a desire to punish the defendant in proportion to the harm inflicted. However relevant such retributive symmetry may be in the criminal law, it has no place in the law of civil damages, at least in the absence of culpability beyond mere negligence.

Accordingly, we conclude that cognitive awareness is a prerequisite to recovery for loss of enjoyment of life. We do not go so far, however, as to require the fact finder to sort out varying degrees of cognition and determine at what level a particular deprivation can be fully appreciated. With respect to pain and suffering, the trial court charged simply that there must be "some level of awareness" in order for plaintiff to recover. We think that this is an appropriate standard for all aspects of nonpecuniary loss. No doubt the standard ignores analytically relevant levels of cognition, but we resist the desire for analytical purity in favor of simplicity. A more complex instruction might give the appearance of greater precision but, given the limits of our understanding of the human mind, it would in reality lead only to greater speculation. We turn next to the question whether loss of enjoyment of life should be considered a category of damages separate from pain and suffering.

IV.

There is no dispute here that the fact finder may, in assessing nonpecuniary damages, consider the effect of the injuries on the plaintiff's capacity to lead a normal life. Traditionally, in this State and elsewhere, this aspect of suffering has not been treated as a separate category of damages; instead, the plaintiff's inability to enjoy life to its fullest has been considered one type of suffering to be factored into a general award for nonpecuniary damages, commonly known as pain and suffering.

Recently, however, there has been an attempt to segregate the suffering associated with physical pain from the mental anguish that stems from the inability to engage in certain activities, and to have juries provide a separate award for each.

Some courts have resisted the effort, primarily on the ground that duplicative and therefore excessive awards would result. Other courts have allowed separate awards, noting that the types of suffering involved are analytically distinguishable. Still other courts have questioned the propriety of the practice but held that, in the particular case, separate awards did not constitute reversible error. . . .

We do not dispute that distinctions can be found or created between the concepts of pain and suffering and loss of enjoyment of life. If the term "suffering" is limited to the emotional response to the sensation of pain, then the emotional response caused by the limitation of life's activities may be considered qualitatively different. But suffering need not be so limited—it can easily encompass the frustration and anguish caused by the inability to participate in activities that once brought pleasure. Traditionally, by treating loss of enjoyment of life as a permissible factor in assessing pain and suffering, courts have given the term this broad meaning.

If we are to depart from this traditional approach and approve a separate award for loss of enjoyment of life, it must be on the basis that such an approach will yield a more accurate evaluation of the compensation due to the plaintiff. We have no doubt that, in general, the total award for nonpecuniary damages would increase if we adopted the rule. That separate awards are advocated by plaintiffs and resisted by defendants is sufficient evidence that larger awards are at stake here. But a larger award does not by itself indicate that the goal of compensation has been better served.

The advocates of separate awards contend that because pain and suffering and loss of enjoyment of life can be distinguished, they must be treated separately if the plaintiff is to be compensated fully for each distinct injury suffered. We disagree. Such an analytical approach may have its place when the subject is pecuniary damages, which can be calculated with some precision. But the estimation of nonpecuniary damages is not amenable to such analytical precision and may, in fact, suffer from its application. Translating human suffering into dollars and cents involves no mathematical formula; it rests, as we have said, on a legal fiction. The figure that emerges is unavoidably distorted by the translation. Application of this murky process to the component parts of nonpecuniary injuries (however analytically distinguishable they may be) cannot make it more accurate. If anything, the distortion will be amplified by repetition.

Thus, we are not persuaded that any salutary purpose would be served by having the jury make separate awards for pain and suffering and loss of enjoyment of life. We are confident, furthermore, that the trial advocate's art is a sufficient guarantee that none of the plaintiff's losses will be ignored by the jury.

The errors in the instructions given to the jury require a new trial on the issue of nonpecuniary damages to be awarded to plaintiff Emma McDougald. Defendants' remaining contentions are either without merit, beyond the scope of our review or are rendered academic by our disposition of the case.

Accordingly, the order of the Appellate Division, insofar as appealed from, should be modified, with costs to defendants, by granting a new trial on the issue of nonpecuniary damages of plaintiff Emma McDougald, and as so modified, affirmed.

TITONE, Judge (dissenting).

The majority's holding represents a compromise position that neither comports with the fundamental principles of tort compensation nor furnishes a satisfactory, logically consistent framework for compensating nonpecuniary loss. Because I conclude that loss of enjoyment of life is an objective damage item, conceptually distinct from conscious pain and suffering, I can find no fault with the trial court's instruction authorizing separate awards and permitting an award for "loss of enjoyment of life" even in the absence of any awareness of that loss on the part of the injured plaintiff. Accordingly, I dissent.

It is elementary that the purpose of awarding tort damages is to compensate the wronged party for the actual loss he or she has sustained. Personal injury damages are awarded "to restore the injured person to the state of health he had prior to his injuries because that is the only way the law knows how to recompense one for personal injuries suffered" (Romeo v. New York City Tr. Auth., 73 Misc. 2d 124, 126, 341 N.Y.S.2d 733; [other citations omitted]). Thus, this court has held that "[t]he person responsible for the injury must respond for all damages resulting directly from and as a natural consequence of the wrongful act" (Steitz v. Gifford, 280 N.Y. 15, 20, 19 N.E.2d 661).

The capacity to enjoy life—by watching one's children grow, participating in recreational activities, and drinking in the many other pleasures that life has to offer—is unquestionably an attribute of an ordinary healthy individual. The loss of that capacity as a result of another's negligent act is at least as serious an impairment as the permanent destruction of a physical function, which has always been treated as a compensable item under traditional tort principles. Indeed, I can imagine no physical loss that is more central to the quality of a tort victim's continuing life than the destruction of the capacity to enjoy that life to the fullest.

Unquestionably, recovery of a damage item such as "pain and suffering" requires a showing of some degree of cognitive capacity. Such a requirement exists for the simple reason that pain and suffering are wholly subjective concepts and cannot exist separate and apart from the human consciousness that experiences them. In contrast, the destruction of an individual's capacity to enjoy life as a result of a crippling injury is an objective fact that does not differ in principle from the permanent loss of an eye or limb. As in the case of a lost limb, an essential characteristic of a healthy human life has been wrongfully taken, and, consequently, the injured party is entitled to a monetary award as a substitute, if, as the majority asserts, the goal of tort compensation is "to restore the injured party, to the extent possible, to the position that would have been occupied had the wrong not occurred" (majority opn., at 254, at 939 of 538 N.Y.S.2d, at 374 of 536 N.E.2d).

Significantly, this equation does not suggest a need to establish the injured's awareness of the loss. The victim's ability to comprehend the degree to which his or her life has been impaired is irrelevant, since, unlike "conscious pain and suffering," the impairment exists independent of the victim's ability to apprehend it. Indeed, the majority reaches the conclusion that a degree of awareness must be shown only after injecting a new element into the equation. Under the majority's formulation, the victim must be aware of the loss because, in addition to being compensatory, the award must have "meaning or utility to the injured person." (Majority opn., at 254, at 940 of 538 N.Y.S.2d, at 375 of 536 N.E.2d.) This additional requirement, however, has no real foundation in law or logic. "Meaning" and "utility" are subjective value judgments that have no place in the law of tort recovery, where the primary goal is to find ways of quantifying, to the extent possible, the worth of various forms of human tragedy.

Moreover, the compensatory nature of a monetary award for loss of enjoyment of life is not altered or rendered punitive by the fact that the unaware injured plaintiff cannot experience the pleasure of having it. The fundamental distinction between punitive and compensatory damages is that the former exceed the amount necessary to replace what the plaintiff lost. As the Court of Appeals for the Second Circuit has observed, "[t]he fact that the compensation [for loss of enjoyment of life] may inure as a practical matter to third parties in a given case does not transform the nature of the damages" (Rufino v. United States, 2nd Cir., 829 F.2d 354, 362).

Ironically, the majority's expressed goal of limiting recovery for non-pecuniary loss to compensation that the injured plaintiff has the capacity to appreciate is directly undercut by the majority's ultimate holding, adopted in the interest of "simplicity," that recovery for loss of enjoyment of life may be had as long as the injured plaintiff has " 'some level of awareness' ", however slight (majority opn., at 255, at 940 of 538 N.Y.S.2d, at 375 of 536 N.E.2d). Manifestly, there are many different forms and levels of awareness, particularly in cases involving brain injury. Further, the type and degree of cognitive functioning necessary to experience "pain and suffering" is certainly of a lower order than that needed to apprehend the loss of the ability to enjoy life in all of its subtleties. Accordingly, the existence of "some level of awareness" on the part of the injured plaintiff says nothing about that plaintiff's ability to derive some comfort from the award or even to appreciate its significance. Hence, that standard does not assure that loss of enjoyment of life damages will be awarded only when they serve "a compensatory purpose," as that term is defined by the majority.

In the final analysis, the rule that the majority has chosen is an arbitrary one, in that it denies or allows recovery on the basis of a criterion that is not truly related to its stated goal. In my view, it is fundamentally unsound, as well as grossly unfair, to deny recovery to those who are completely without cognitive capacity while permitting it for those with a mere spark of awareness, regardless of the latter's ability to appreciate either the loss sustained or the benefits of the monetary award offered in compensation. In both instances, the injured plaintiff is in essentially the same position, and an award that is punitive as to one is equally punitive as to the other. Of course, since I do not subscribe to the majority's conclusion that an award to an unaware plaintiff is punitive, I would have no difficulty permitting recovery to both classes of plaintiffs.

Having concluded that the injured plaintiff's awareness should not be a necessary precondition to recovery for loss of enjoyment of life, I also have no difficulty going on to conclude that loss of enjoyment of life is a distinct damage item which is recoverable separate and apart from the award for conscious pain and suffering. The majority has rejected separate recovery, in part because it apparently perceives some overlap between the two damage categories and in part because it believes that the goal of enhancing the precision of jury awards for nonpecuniary loss would not be advanced. However, the overlap the majority perceives exists only if one assumes, as the majority evidently has (see, majority opn., at 256-257, at 940-942 of 538 N.Y.S.2d, at 375-377 of 536 N.E.2d), that the "loss of enjoyment" category of damages is designed to compensate only for "*the emotional response* caused by the limitation of life's activities" and "*the frustration and anguish caused by* the inability to participate in activities that once brought pleasure" (emphasis added), both of which are highly *subjective* concepts.

In fact, while "pain and suffering compensates the victim for the physical and mental discomfort caused by the injury; . . . loss of enjoyment of life compensates the victim for the limitations on the person's life created by the injury," a distinctly objective loss (Thompson v.

National R.R. Passenger Corp., [6th Cir., 621 F.2d 814, 824, *cert. denied,* 449 U.S. 1035, 101 S. Ct. 611, 66 L. Ed. 2d 497]). In other words, while the victim's "emotional response" and "frustration and anguish" are elements of the award for pain and suffering, the "limitation of life's activities" and the "inability to participate in activities" that the majority identifies are recoverable under the "loss of enjoyment of life" rubric. Thus, there is no real overlap, and no real basis for concern about potentially duplicative awards where, as here, there is a properly instructed jury.

Finally, given the clear distinction between the two categories of non-pecuniary damages, I cannot help but assume that permitting separate awards for conscious pain and suffering and loss of enjoyment of life would contribute to accuracy and precision in thought in the jury's deliberations on the issue of damages. . . . In light of the concrete benefit to be gained by compelling the jury to differentiate between the specific objective and subjective elements of the plaintiff's nonpecuniary loss, I find unpersuasive the majority's reliance on vague concerns about potential distortion owing to the inherently difficult task of computing the value of intangible loss. My belief in the jury system, and in the collective wisdom of the deliberating jury, leads me to conclude that we may safely leave that task in the jurors' hands.

For all of these reasons, I approve of the approach that the trial court adopted in its charge to the jury. Accordingly, I would affirm the order below affirming the judgment.

B. Punitive Damages

Page 286.   *After* Taylor v. Superior Court, *add the following new case:*

Owens-Illinois, Inc. v. Zenobia
325 Md. 420, 601 A.2d 633 (1992)

Opinion by ELDRIDGE, J. [This was a suit for damages alleged to have been caused by asbestos manufactured by the defendants. The jury awarded punitive damages against some defendants, including Owens-Illinois. The intermediate appellate court affirmed the punitive damage award against Owens-Illinois, who appealed that issue, among others.]

We issued a writ of certiorari in these cases to consider several important questions [including] some of the principles governing awards of punitive damages in tort cases. . . .

IV.

In granting the petitions for a writ of certiorari in these cases, this Court issued an order requesting that the briefs and argument encompass the following issue:

> [W]hat should be the correct standard under Maryland law for the allowance of punitive damages in negligence and products liability cases, i.e., gross negligence, actual malice, or some other standard.

[I]n recent years there has been a proliferation of claims for punitive damages in tort cases, and awards of punitive damages have often been extremely high. . . .

Accompanying this increase in punitive damages claims, awards and amounts of awards, is renewed criticism of the concept of punitive damages in a tort system designed primarily to compensate injured parties for harm. In Maryland the criticism has been partly fueled and justified because juries are provided with imprecise and uncertain characterizations of the type of conduct which will expose a defendant to a potential award of punitive damages. Accordingly, we shall (1) examine these characterizations of a defendant's conduct in light of the historic objectives of punitive damages, (2) more precisely define the nature of conduct potentially subject to a punitive damages award in non-intentional tort cases, and (3) heighten the standard of proof required of a plaintiff seeking an award of punitive damages.

These cases, along with two others heard by us on the same day, directly raise the problem of what basic standard of wrongful conduct should be used for the allowance of punitive damages in negligence actions generally, and in products liability actions based on either negligence or on strict liability. The jury in these cases received the following instruction on punitive damages: "Implied malice, which the plaintiffs have to prove in order to recover punitive damages in this case, requires a finding by you of a wanton disposition, grossly irresponsible to the rights of others, extreme recklessness and utter disregard for the rights of others." . . . [The] court required the plaintiffs to show by a preponderance of evidence that the defendants acted with "implied" rather than "actual" malice. That is, the plaintiffs were not required to show that the defendants' conduct was characterized by evil motive, intent to injure, fraud, or actual knowledge of the defective nature of the products coupled with a deliberate disregard of the consequences. Instead, the plaintiffs were required to show only that the defendants' conduct was grossly negligent.

The standard applied by the trial court . . . results from, and consequently requires re-examination of, some of the decisions of this Court relating to punitive damages. . . .

B. . . .

In 1972 this Court, for the first time in a non-intentional tort action, allowed an award of punitive damages based upon implied malice. The Court . . . allow[ed] the plaintiff to recover punitive damages upon a showing that the defendant was guilty of "gross negligence," which was defined as a "wanton or reckless disregard for human life." . . .

The gross negligence standard has led to inconsistent results and frustration of the purposes of punitive damages in non-intentional tort cases. . . .

In the face of "a literal explosion of punitive damage law and practice," many states have acted to define more accurately the type of conduct which can form the basis for a punitive damages award. In Tuttle v. Raymond, 494 A.2d 1353 (Me. 1985), the Supreme Judicial Court of Maine reviewed its law on punitive damages. The implied malice standard applied by the lower courts in *Tuttle* allowed recovery of punitive damages upon a showing that the defendant's conduct was "wanton, malicious, reckless or grossly negligent." 494 A.2d at 1360. The court rejected this standard, stating (494 A.2d at 1361): " 'Gross' negligence simply covers too broad and too vague an area of behavior, resulting in an unfair and inefficient use of the doctrine of punitive damages. . . . A similar problem exists with allowing punitive damages based merely upon 'reckless' conduct. 'To sanction punitive damages solely upon the basis of conduct characterized as heedless disregard of the consequences would be to allow virtually limitless imposition of punitive damages.' " The Maine court went on to point out that the implied malice standard "overextends the availability of punitive damages" and consequently "dulls the potentially keen edge of the doctrine as an effective deterrent of truly reprehensible conduct." Ibid. . . .

As previously indicated, arbitrary and inconsistent application of the standard for awarding punitive damages frustrates the dual purposes of punishment and deterrence. Implied malice as that term has been used, with its various and imprecise formulations, fosters this uncertainty. As pointed out by Professor Ellis, (D. Ellis, Fairness and Efficiency in the Law of Punitive Damages, 56 S. Cal. L. Rev. 1, 52-53 (1982)): "[T]he law of punitive damages is characterized by a high degree of uncertainty that stems from the use of a multiplicity of vague, overlapping terms. . . . Accordingly, there is little reason to believe that only deserving defendants are punished, or that fair notice of punishable conduct is provided." . . .

The implied malice test . . . has been overbroad in its application and has resulted in inconsistent jury verdicts involving similar facts. It provides little guidance for individuals and companies to enable them to predict behavior that will either trigger or avoid punitive damages liability, and it undermines the deterrent effect of these awards. . . . In a non-intentional tort action, the trier of facts may not award punitive damages unless the plaintiff has established that the defendant's conduct was characterized by evil motive, intent to injure, ill will, or fraud, i.e., "actual malice." . . .

E.

The defendant Owens-Illinois and some amici have argued that, in order for a jury to consider a punitive damages award, a plaintiff should be required to establish by clear and convincing evidence that the defendant's conduct was characterized by actual malice. . . .

A growing majority of states requires that a plaintiff prove the defendant's malicious conduct by clear and convincing evidence before punitive damages can be considered. Many states have adopted the clear and convincing standard by statute. Other states have adopted the standard by judicial decisions. . . .

Use of a clear and convincing standard of proof will help to insure that punitive damages are properly awarded. We hold that this heightened standard is appropriate in the assessment of punitive damages because of their penal nature and potential for debilitating harm. Consequently, in any tort case a plaintiff must establish by clear and convincing evidence the basis for an award of punitive damages. . . .

[The concurring opinion of McAuliffe, J. is omitted.]

Concurring and dissenting opinion by Bell, J. . . .

I part company with the majority on the question of what is the appropriate standard for determining the cases in which punitive damages are appropriate. While I have no quarrel with requiring that, in some cases, "actual malice," characterized as "evil motive," "intent to injure," "ill will," "fraud," or, in the case of products liability actions, "actual knowledge of the defective nature of the product, coupled with a deliberate disregard of the consequences," be shown, I am opposed to excising from the standard the concept . . . : "wanton or reckless disregard for human life," sometimes characterized as "gross negligence." That standard, now the old one, is a floor, not a ceiling; it sets a minimum requirement, not a maximum. Therefore, if a defendant acts with "actual malice," however characterized, he or she will be subject to an award of punitive damages under the old standard. On the other hand, by adopting the "actual malice" standard, the majority does much more than excise a useless phrase, it places outside the scope of punitive damages eligibility numerous deserving cases, differing from cases that remain punitive damages eligible only in the subjective element. That change simply goes too far.

The perception is that more claims for punitive damages, involving conduct so diverse that predictability and, therefore, the ability to choose the proper conduct and avoid being culpable, than were justified, were being brought and allowed that the purposes of punitive damages were being undermined. The changes proposed are for the purpose of making the awards more uniform and consistent with the historical bases for punitive damages awards: punishment and deterrence. The purposes of punitive damages are better served, it has been determined, by requiring a more stringent standard for assessing punitive damages and by requiring a greater burden of proof. To be sure, one of the goals of today's decision is to set a higher threshold for punitive damages eligibility. That is accomplished by changing the burden of proof, that clearly will exclude some undeserving cases, no doubt, a large number, even applying the old standard. But, by both changing the burden of proof and the standard, an even greater percentage of deserving cases, heretofore eligible for punitive damages awards is affected. Indeed, by so doing, not only is the threshold raised, but excluded is an entire category of cases, non-intentional torts, involving, in many instances, injuries of greater severity than in cases that still qualify and, thus, not necessarily those least deserving of an award of punitive damages. And the distinction causing the exclusion is the subjective intent of the defendant. While I can agree, as I have previously indicated, to raising the threshold by raising the level of the proof required, I cannot agree that punitive damages should be awarded only in cases of "actual malice," where there is a subjective intent element. In cases where there is no actual malice, the totality of the circumstances may reveal conduct on the part of a defendant that is just as heinous as the conduct motivated by that actual malice and, so, for all intents and purposes is the same.

Although not intentional, i.e., willful, conduct, nevertheless, may be outrageousness and extreme in the context in which it occurs, and may produce injuries commensurate with those caused by intentional conduct. In other words, conduct may be so reckless and outrageous as to be the equivalent of intentional conduct. . . .

Permitting punitive damages when one acts with actual malice, but not when, given the totality of the circumstances, that same person acts in total disregard for the safety of others has no reasoned basis.

Consider the following example. A hot water pipe bursts in a crowded apartment complex quite near an open area upon which young people are playing baseball. A repair team dispatched to make repairs observes young people playing baseball nearby. It also sees that the area of the affected pipe is in easy reach of a baseball hit to the outfield. Nevertheless, they dig a hole, but, being unable to proceed due to the temperature of the water, suspend operations. Although aware of the young people playing in the area, they leave without warning them of the hole or its contents or in any way marking or obstructing the hole. One of the outfielders, having chased and caught a ball hit to the outfield, falls into the hole and is severely injured.

Under the new standard, if it could be proved that a member of the repair team harbored ill will toward the outfielder and, in the back of his mind, entertained a hope that the outfielder, or one of the other players, would fall in the unattended hole, then, in addition to compensable damages, the outfielder could recover punitive damages. On the other hand, if none of the members of the repair team knew any of the ball players and, in fact, harbored no evil motive at all, no punitive damages could be recovered, notwithstanding that they acted, given the circumstances, in total disregard of the safety of the ballplayers. I can see no reasoned difference between these scenarios. The state of mind of the individual simply is not so important a factor as to permit recovery in one case and not in the other.

I am satisfied that allowing punitive damages for "wanton and reckless conduct," . . . serves the purposes of punishment and deterrence. Gross negligence, outrageous conduct, etc. cannot be defined in a vacuum. To have meaning, the terms must be viewed in a factual context. The conduct described in the example is not only outrageous and extraordinary, it is the sine qua non of reckless conduct. Such conduct should be punished. And that scenario presents a striking example of the kind of conduct a defendant must not engage in if he or she is to avoid paying punitive damages. The example I have proffered is not the only one that can be posited. There are hundreds of such cases. The long and short of it is that changing the standard for punitive damages will eliminate numbers of cases, in which, heretofore, punitive damages would have been appropriate and those cases now are eliminated not because their facts are not egregious enough to justify such an award but because other, less serious, and perhaps, undeserving, cases may also qualify for such damages. With all due respect, that is not a sufficiently good reason to change the rules of the game.

Insulating a defendant from an award of punitive damages except when he or she acts with actual malice, meaning with an evil intent, ill will, with intent to injure, or to defraud, provides a disincentive for that defendant to act reasonably. Since, from the standpoint of a defendant's pocketbook, it makes no difference in the award of damages, whether he or she is negligent or grossly negligent, that is, his or her conduct is extreme to a point just short of being intentional, requiring that defendant to pay compensatory damages for the victims's injuries is not likely to have a deterrent effect; it is not likely to cause him or her to consider, not to mention, change, his or her conduct. . . .

Page 290. After the third full paragraph, add the following new text:

The constitutionality of statutes which call for a payment of part of a punitive damage award to the state has been litigated in a number of cases. Holding the statutory scheme to be constitutional is Gordon v. State, 585 So. 2d 1033 (Fla. App. 1991). The statute called for 60 percent of the award to be paid to either the Public Assistance Trust Fund or the General Revenue Fund. The plaintiff argued, unsuccessfully, that the statute unconstitutionally took private property. A similar constitutional claim had greater success in Kirk v. Denver Publishing Co., 818 P.2d 262 (Colo. 1991), in which the court held that a statute requiring one-third of the plaintiff's exemplary damage award be paid to the state's general fund was an unconstitutional taking of property without just compensation.

Page 290. At end of page, add the following new case:

Pacific Mutual Life Insurance Co. v. Haslip
111 S. Ct. 1032 (1991)

Justice BLACKMUN delivered the opinion of the Court.
This case is yet another that presents a challenge to a punitive damages award.

I

In 1981, Lemmie L. Ruffin, Jr., was an Alabama-licensed agent for petitioner Pacific Mutual Life Insurance Company. [Ruffin collected premiums for a medical insurance policy from the municipality for which respondents worked, but did not forward them to Pacific Mutual. Unknown to the respondents, Pacific Mutual cancelled the policy.]

Respondent Haslip was hospitalized on January 23, 1982. She incurred hospital and physician's charges. Because the hospital could not confirm health coverage, it required Haslip, upon her discharge, to make a payment upon her bill. Her physician, when he was not paid, placed her account with a collection agency. The agency obtained a judgment against Haslip and her credit was adversely affected.

In May 1982, respondents filed this suit, naming as defendants Pacific Mutual . . . and Ruffin, individually and as a proprietorship. . . . Damages for fraud were claimed. The case against Pacific Mutual was submitted to the jury under a theory of respondeat superior.

[After a jury verdict awarding punitive damages, the trial judge entered a judgment for punitive damages against Pacific Mutual and Ruffin.]

Pacific Mutual . . . brought the case here. It challenged punitive damages in Alabama as the product of unbridled jury discretion and as violative of its due process rights.

III

This Court . . . on a number of occasions in recent years [has] expressed doubts about the constitutionality of certain punitive damages awards.

In Browning-Ferris Industries of Vermont, Inc. v. Kelco Disposal, Inc., 492 U.S. 257, 109 S. Ct. 2909, 106 L. Ed. 2d 219 (1989), . . . the majority held that the Excessive Fines Clause of the Eighth Amendment did not apply to a punitive damages award in a civil case between private parties. . . .

IV

Two preliminary and overlapping due process arguments raised by Pacific Mutual deserve attention before we reach the principal issue in controversy. Did Ruffin act within the scope of his apparent authority as an agent of Pacific Mutual? If so, may Pacific Mutual be held responsible for Ruffin's fraud on a theory of respondeat superior? . . .

The jury found that Ruffin was acting as an employee of Pacific Mutual when he defrauded respondents. The Supreme Court of Alabama did not disturb that finding. There is no occasion for us to question it, for it is amply supported by the record. . . .

Alabama's common-law rule is that a corporation is liable for both compensatory and punitive damages for fraud of its employee effected within the scope of his employment. We cannot say that this does not rationally advance the State's interest in minimizing fraud. . . .

Imposing exemplary damages on the corporation when its agent commits intentional fraud creates a strong incentive for vigilance by those in a position "to guard substantially against the evil to be prevented." Louis Pizitz Dry Goods Co. v. Yeldell, 274 U.S. 112, 116, 47 S. Ct. 509, 510, 71 L. Ed. 952 (1927). If an insurer were liable for such damages only upon proof that it was at fault independently, it would have an incentive to minimize oversight of its agents. Imposing liability without independent fault deters fraud more than a less stringent rule. It therefore rationally advances the State's goal. We cannot say this is a violation of Fourteenth Amendment due process. . . .

V . . .

Under the traditional common-law approach, the amount of the punitive award is initially determined by a jury instructed to consider the gravity of the wrong and the need to deter similar wrongful conduct. The jury's determination is then reviewed by trial and appellate courts to ensure that it is reasonable.

This Court more than once has approved the common-law method for assessing punitive awards. . . .

So far as we have been able to determine, every state and federal court that has considered the question has ruled that the common-law method for assessing punitive damages does not in itself violate due process. . . . In view of this consistent history, we cannot say that the common-law method for assessing punitive damages is so inherently unfair as to deny due process and be per se unconstitutional. " 'If a thing has been practiced for two hundred years by common consent, it will need a strong case for the Fourteenth Amendment to affect it.' " Sun Oil Co. v. Wortman, 486 U.S. 717, 730, 108 S. Ct. 2117, 2126, 100 L. Ed. 2d 743 (1988), quoting Jackman v. Rosenbaum Co., 260 U.S. 22, 31, 43 S. Ct. 9, 10, 67 L. Ed. 107 (1922). . . .

This, however, is not the end of the matter. It would be just as inappropriate to say that, because punitive damages have been recognized for so long, their imposition is never unconstitutional. . . . We note once again our concern about punitive damages that "run wild." Having said that, we conclude that our task today is to determine whether the Due Process Clause renders the punitive damages award in this case constitutionally unacceptable.

VI

One must concede that unlimited jury discretion—or unlimited judicial discretion for that matter—in the fixing of punitive damages may invite extreme results that jar one's constitutional sensibilities. We need not, and indeed we cannot, draw a mathematical bright line between the constitutionally acceptable and the constitutionally unacceptable that would fit every case. We can say, however, that general concerns of reasonableness and adequate guidance from the court when the case is tried to a jury properly enter into the constitutional calculus. With these concerns in mind, we review the constitutionality of the punitive damages awarded in this case.

We conclude that the punitive damages assessed by the jury against Pacific Mutual were not violative of the Due Process Clause of the Fourteenth Amendment. It is true, of course, that under Alabama law, as under the law of most States, punitive damages are imposed for purposes of retribution and deterrence. . . . But this in itself does not provide the answer. We move, then, to the points of specific attack.

1. We have carefully reviewed the instructions to the jury. By these instructions . . . the trial court expressly described for the jury the purpose of punitive damages, namely, "not to compensate the plaintiff for any injury" but "to punish the defendant" and "for the added purpose of protecting the public by [deterring] the defendant and others from doing such wrong in the future." App. 105-106. Any evidence of Pacific Mutual's wealth was excluded from the trial in accord with Alabama law.

To be sure, the instructions gave the jury significant discretion in its determination of punitive damages. But that discretion was not unlimited. It was confined to deterrence and retribution, the state policy concerns sought to be advanced. And if punitive damages were to be awarded, the jury "must take into consideration the character and the degree of the wrong as shown by the evidence and necessity of preventing similar wrong." App. 106. The instructions thus enlightened the jury as to the punitive damages' nature and purpose, identified the damages as punishment for civil wrongdoing of the kind involved, and explained that their imposition was not compulsory. These instructions, we believe, reasonably accommodated Pacific Mutual's interest in rational decisionmaking and Alabama's interest in meaningful individualized assessment of appropriate deterrence and retribution. The discretion allowed under Alabama law in determining punitive damages is no greater than that pursued in many familiar areas of the law as, for example, deciding "the best interests of the child," or "reasonable care," or "due diligence," or appropriate compensation for pain and suffering or mental anguish. As long as the discretion is exercised within reasonable constraints, due process is satisfied.

2. Before the trial in this case took place, the Supreme Court of Alabama had established post-trial procedures for scrutinizing punitive

awards. In Hammond v. City of Gadsden, 493 So. 2d 1374 (1986), it stated that trial courts are "to reflect in the record the reasons for interfering with a jury verdict, or refusing to do so, on grounds of excessiveness of the damages." Id., at 1379. Among the factors deemed "appropriate for the trial court's consideration" are the "culpability of the defendant's conduct," the "desirability of discouraging others from similar conduct," the "impact upon the parties," and "other factors, such as the impact on innocent third parties." Ibid. The *Hammond* test ensures meaningful and adequate review by the trial court whenever a jury has fixed the punitive damages.

3. By its review of punitive awards, the Alabama Supreme Court provides an additional check on the jury's or trial court's discretion. It first undertakes a comparative analysis. It then applies the detailed substantive standards it has developed for evaluating punitive awards. In particular, it makes its review to ensure that the award does "not exceed an amount that will accomplish society's goals of punishment and deterrence." Green Oil Co. v. Hornsby, 539 So. 2d 218, 222 (1989); Wilson v. Dukona Corp., 547 So. 2d 70, 73 (1989). This appellate review makes certain that the punitive damages are reasonable in their amount and rational in light of their purpose to punish what has occurred and to deter its repetition.

Also before its ruling in the present case, the Supreme Court of Alabama had elaborated and refined the *Hammond* criteria for determining whether a punitive award is reasonably related to the goals of deterrence and retribution. It was announced that the following could be taken into consideration in determining whether the award was excessive or inadequate: (a) whether there is a reasonable relationship between the punitive damages award and the harm likely to result from the defendant's conduct as well as the harm that actually has occurred; (b) the degree of reprehensibility of the defendant's conduct, the duration of that conduct, the defendant's awareness, any concealment, and the existence and frequency of similar past conduct; (c) the profitability to the defendant of the wrongful conduct and the desirability of removing that profit and of having the defendant also sustain a loss; (d) the "financial position" of the defendant; (e) all the costs of litigation; (f) the imposition of criminal sanctions on the defendant for its conduct, these to be taken in mitigation; and (g) the existence of other civil awards against the defendant for the same conduct, these also to be taken in mitigation.

The application of these standards, we conclude, imposes a sufficiently definite and meaningful constraint on the discretion of Alabama fact finders in awarding punitive damages. The Alabama Supreme Court's post-verdict review ensures that punitive damages awards are not grossly out of proportion to the severity of the offense and have some understandable relationship to compensatory damages. While punitive damages in Alabama may embrace such factors as the heinousness of the civil wrong, its effect upon the victim, the likelihood of its recurrence, and the extent of defendant's wrongful gain, the fact finder must be guided by more than the defendant's net worth. Alabama plaintiffs do not enjoy a windfall because they have the good fortune to have a defendant with a deep pocket.

We are aware that the punitive damages award in this case is more than 4 times the amount of compensatory damages, is more than 200 times the out-of-pocket expenses of respondent Haslip. . . . Imprisonment, however, could also be required of an individual in the criminal context. While the monetary comparisons are wide and, indeed, may be close to the line, the award here did not lack objective criteria. We conclude, after careful consideration, that in this case it does not cross the line into the area of constitutional impropriety. Accordingly, Pacific Mutual's due process challenge must be, and is, rejected.

The judgment of the Supreme Court of Alabama is affirmed. It is so ordered.

[The concurring opinions of Justices SCALIA and KENNEDY and the dissenting opinion of Justice O'CONNOR are omitted.]

The lower courts have not viewed *Haslip* as foreclosing inquiry into the constitutionality of punitive damage awards. See, e.g., Mattison v. Dallas Carrier Corp., 947 F.2d 95 (4th Cir. 1991). The court held that the South Carolina punitive damage regime was unconstitutional because it left no guidance to the jury in determining the amount of the award. The court held that the jury must, as a matter of constitutional law, be told to consider the following (947 F.2d at 110):

> (1) Relationship to harm caused: Any penalty imposed should take into account the reprehensibility of the conduct, the harm caused, the defendant's awareness of the conduct's wrongfulness, the duration of the conduct, and any concealment. Thus any penalty imposed should bear a relationship to the nature and extent of the conduct and the harm caused, including the compensatory damage award made by the jury.
>
> (2) Other penalties for the conduct: Any penalty imposed should take into account as a mitigating factor any other penalty that may have been imposed or which may be imposed for the conduct involved, including any criminal or civil penalty or any other punitive damages award arising out of the same conduct.
>
> (3) Improper profits and plaintiff's costs: The amount of any penalty may

focus on depriving the defendant of profits derived from the improper conduct and on awarding the costs to the plaintiff of prosecuting the claim.

(4) Limitation based on ability to pay: Any penalty must be limited to punishment and thus may not effect economic bankruptcy. To this end, the ability of the defendant to pay any punitive award entered should be considered.

Part III

Substantive Bases of Liability

Chapter 6

Negligence

B. The General Standard

Page 346. At bottom of page, add the following new case and text:

Dobson v. Louisiana Power and Light Co.
567 So. 2d 569 (La. 1990)

DENNIS, Justice. This is a wrongful death action, pursuant to Louisiana Civil Code article 2315.2, by the surviving spouse and five minor children of a tree trimmer, Dwane L. Dobson, who was electrocuted on April 24, 1985 when his metallically reinforced safety rope contacted an uninsulated 8,000 volt electric power distribution line. The trial court awarded the widow and her children $1,034,054.50 in damages, after finding the deceased free of fault and holding the Louisiana Power & Light Company liable in negligence for failure to maintain its right of way, insulate its high voltage distribution line, or give adequate warnings of the line's dangerous nature. The court of appeal affirmed the decree as to the power company's negligence, but reversed in part, reducing the plaintiff's recovery by 70% based on a finding that the deceased had been guilty of fault to that degree. Dobson v. Louisiana Power & Light Co., 550 So. 2d 1334 (La. App. 1st Cir. 1989).

The facts, as the trial judge found them, were as follows: Dwane L. Dobson, a 29 year old tree trimmer, was electrocuted while attempting to remove a pine tree from the backyard of a house owned by a Mrs. Davidge in Hammond, Louisiana. The tree was located near the rear property line, which was adjacent to a right of way for LP & L's uninsulated high voltage distribution lines serving an apartment complex. Dobson was wearing a safety line he had made by inserting a metal wire inside a 13 foot nylon rope. He used the safety line to lash himself to the tree while cutting with his chain saw, and he had inserted the wire in the rope to prevent it from being accidentally severed by the saw. Just prior to the accident, Dobson had cut a section from the top of the tree and had lowered it with the help of his coworkers below. As he descended to cut another section, his safety line touched one of the uninsulated distribution lines and he was electrocuted.

The LP & L high voltage distribution lines behind Mrs. Davidge's property were installed in 1968 to carry electricity 315 feet from Wardline Road to the University Apartments. The lines were elevated from the road to a point behind the Davidge house and placed underground from there to the apartments. LP & L originally intended that the entire span be buried to serve other commercial purposes but those developments did not occur.

Mrs. Davidge complained many times to LP & L about hazards created by the condition of the elevated lines and the right of way behind her house. She complained about transformers blowing up, limbs falling into the wires, fires caused by trees falling on the lines, and having to call the city fire department to extinguish the blazes. Some time prior to the accident she asked LP & L to remove a pine tree behind her house because it was "spindly" and overhanging the power lines. This was the same tree she later hired Dobson to remove. LP & L rejected her requests because the base of the tree was in her backyard and not in LP & L's right of way. LP & L never came to inspect or remove the tree. During this time LP & L suffered from the lack of adequate funds to properly trim trees in its rights of way in the Hammond area. Also, LP & L had no regular team or program devoted exclusively to the inspection of its lines and rights of way but relied on its employees to watch for dangers as they performed other duties.

Dobson had started his tree trimming service several months before his death. He had no formal training but was learning from hard work, experience and talking with other local tree trimmers. After he accidentally damaged a single residence service line at another location in Hammond, an LP & L representative informed him that LP & L would lower such single unit service lines to facilitate tree trimming and that LP & L would assist him generally in the future. The LP & L representative did not inform Dobson that some of its major distribution lines, unlike its single residence service lines, were uninsulated or that LP & L would lower or deenergize major distribution lines for his tree trimming jobs. The day before Dobson's death he was successful in getting LP & L to lower a single consumer service line during his work. However, because Dobson had no reason to believe that LP & L would have lowered or deenergized the major distribution lines serving the apartment complex to facilitate his removal of the pine tree for Mrs. Davidge, he did not request LP & L to do so.

The trial judge concluded that LP & L was guilty of several negligent acts or omissions that caused the fatal accident: Despite LP & L's constructive and actual knowledge of the dangers created by its uninsulated lines and right of way conditions, it failed to perform adequate inspections of its electric lines, trim or remove the tree or trees creating the hazard, provide insulated covering of dangerous parts of the lines, or place adequate warnings of the high voltage electricity on or near its uncovered wires. Furthermore, the trial judge found that even though LP & L had actual knowledge that Dobson was an inexperienced tree trimmer who would be working near its uninsulated distribution lines in Hammond, the company failed to warn Dobson of the dangers associated with its high voltage distribution lines. With respect to Dobson, the trial judge ultimately found that he did not know of or appreciate the special danger created by the uninsulated overhead high voltage distribution lines; and further that Dobson was not negligent because he was unaware of the extreme danger.

The trial court's purely factual findings were free of clear or manifest error. For example, its resolution of the most hotly contested factual issue—whether Dobson was unaware that the distribution lines were not insulated—was based on reasonable inferences of fact and evaluations of credibility.

As an important background fact, the evidence clearly established the great disparity of danger between "distribution" lines and "service" lines. "Distribution" lines are uninsulated wires used to deliver very high voltage electricity—as much as 8,000 volts—throughout the community. In contrast, "service" lines are insulated with nonconductive covering and used to transfer much lower voltage electricity from distribution lines to individual dwellings. Despite this great difference in danger, distribution lines carry no special markings or warnings but are black in color and similar in appearance to service lines. Dobson's coworkers and relatives testified that they thought the distribution lines were insulated both because they appeared to have black covering and because birds and squirrels traversed them without harm. Thus, the trier of fact reasonably could have inferred that the distribution line's appearance belied its lethally uninsulated nature and made it difficult for an untrained person to appreciate its fatally dangerous character.

The evidence was in conflict regarding whether Dobson had knowledge of the dangers of the distribution lines. On the one hand, Dobson's coworkers and relatives testified that he was ignorant of the deadly conductivity of the distribution lines, and the plaintiffs' experts were of the opinion that his actions prior to the accident indicated that he was unaware of the danger. On the other hand, a power company trouble-shooter testified that he had talked to Dobson on two occasions prior to the accident and that it was his habit to warn tree trimmers of such dangers and to offer to drop or deenergize power lines for them. In the aggregate, however, the trouble-shooter's testimony was equivocal as to whether he had warned Dobson, specifically, of the absence of insulation on distribution lines or had definitely offered to deenergize them for Dobson's operations.[37a] Moreover, these conversations occurred only be-

37a. Contrary to Justice Cole's assertion in his dissent, Mr. Cavaretta's testimony is not "uncontradicted"; in addition to being in conflict with other evidence in the record, Mr. Cavaretta's testimony was "self-contradictory." See the following excerpts:

> Q: [Y]ou cannot testify that you specifically warned Dwane Dobson or explained to him, any of the hazards in working next to or near the distribution primary voltage lines can you?
> A: Sir, I make it a habit, specifically, to warn any tree trimmer of the hazards of electrical power around trees. I've made it a habit ever since I became a service man. . . .
> Q: [Y]ou don't remember specifically warning Dwane or explaining to him any of the hazards in working next to or near the distribution primary voltage lines?
> A: The only thing that I do remember is that on one of those two occasions that I had a chance to talk to Dwane Dobson, was that the question came up, was that we would not drop primary voltage distribution wires. And I told him in so many words, that it was on a individual basis, as to whether we would drop 'em, at that time, or if we would deem it necessary for our people—our right of way people, to go out and remove these trees to a point that he, or whoever was cutting trees, could remove 'em safely. I basically remember that.
>
> Q: And at page twenty-eight of your deposition, line five: I asked you this question: Did you tell him, explain to him, or warn him of any of the hazards in working next to or near a distribution, primary voltage lines?
>   And your answer on line nine, says: For me to tell you exactly that I did, I can't do that. On a routine basis, when I talked with three trimmers, I try to make it a habit to warn these people that there is danger, and to be very careful; if they have any problems, please contact us first, so that we can help them as much as we can. Was that the way you answered that question—at your deposition?
> A: Yes sir.
>
> Q: [W]hen you dropped those two lines the day before he was killed, you don't remember having a conversation with Dwane, and if you did have a conversation with him, you don't remember any part of it, isn't that true?
> A: That's true.
>
> Q: Mr. Cavaretta, you told Dwane Dobson, that generally, you would basically assist him in anyway possible on anything? And you never specifically told him about primary voltage, because you were never asked, or never told that Dwane Dobson was going to work on any primary, or around any primary voltage, and he never asked you about it, isn't that true?
> A: Sir, he did ask me.
> Q: You're absolutely sure of that?
> A: No sir, I'm not.

Thus, even though some of Mr. Cavaretta's testimony may be interpreted as indicating that he warned Dobson of the dangers of primary distribution wires, his entire, inconsistent testimony casts serious doubt on such a finding. In no case can it be said that Cavaretta's testimony by itself is a clear indication of the degree of Dobson's knowledge. We believe that the record as a whole indicates that the trial court's inferences and credibility judgments as to Dobson's lack of knowledge were reasonable.

Therefore, under the rule of Canter v. Koehring, 283 So. 2d 716 (La. 1973), the trial court's finding should not be disturbed.

cause Dobson had accidentally knocked down service lines at two dwellings and the company representative had come to inspect the damage and to repair the service lines. Thus, the service line incidents involved only property damage to insulated service lines and had no direct relationship to the risk of personal injury or death created by uninsulated distribution lines or the need for precautions against such hazards. Additionally, there is no evidence that prior to the accident Dobson had ever had any first hand experience with uninsulated distribution lines or had received any demonstrative instruction in how to identify and guard against their dangers. Therefore, the evidence is easily susceptible to the reasonable inference that the trouble-shooter's discussions with Dobson focused primarily on the prevention of future damage to the company's insulated service lines rather than on Dobson's safety while working around uninsulated distribution lines. This inference bolsters the trial court's reasonable decision to credit the testimony of the plaintiffs' witnesses to the effect that Dobson was unaware of the extreme danger of the uninsulated distribution lines before the accident. Where there are factual issues upon which the evidence is in conflict, reasonable evaluations of credibility and reasonable inferences of fact by the trial court should not be disturbed on review.

[The Court's treatment of plaintiff's contributory negligence is omitted.]

We see no error in the Court of Appeal's conclusion that LP & L was guilty of negligence that caused Dobson's death and should be held at least partially responsible for the damages occasioned by the accident. . . .

[The court allocates partial fault to the plaintiff's decedent and reduces the recovery by forty percent. Concurring and dissenting opinions are omitted.]

———————

Can you distinguish this case from *Clinton* (casebook p. 383)? Why should the plaintiff in *Dobson* recover and the plaintiff in *Clinton* lose as a matter of law?

D.   Modification of the General Standard Arising Out of Special Relationships Between the Parties

1.   Responsibility of Possessors of Land for the Safety of Trespassers, Licensees, and Invitees

Page 460.   Before Problem 21, add the following new case:

Ward v. K mart Corporation
136 Ill. 2d 132, 554 N.E.2d 223 (1990)

Justice RYAN delivered the opinion of the court:

Plaintiff, George Ward, sued in the circuit court of Champaign County, seeking damages for injuries he sustained when he walked into a concrete post located just outside a customer entrance to a department store operated by defendant, K mart Corporation. At the time of the injury, plaintiff was carrying a large mirror which he had purchased from defendant. Following a jury trial and a verdict in favor of plaintiff, the circuit court entered judgment for defendant notwithstanding the jury's verdict on the ground that defendant had no duty to warn plaintiff of, or otherwise protect him from, the risk of colliding with the post. The appellate court, with one justice dissenting, affirmed the judgment n.o.v. and held that defendant owed no duty to plaintiff under the circumstances of this case because defendant could not reasonably have been expected to foresee that plaintiff, while carrying the mirror, would fail to see or remember the post, which was an obvious condition on defendant's premises, and which plaintiff had previously encountered. Plaintiff appeals to this court. We hold that defendant's duty to exercise reasonable care extended to the risk that one of its customers would collide with the post while leaving the store carrying a large, bulky item. Accordingly, we reverse and remand.

Defendant operates a department store in Champaign, Illinois. The store contains a home improvements department. Toward the northern end of the east side of the store is an overhead, garage-type door. Over this door is a large sign which states "Home Center." Facing this large door from the outside, approximately four feet to the right, there is a smaller door approximately 36 inches wide. On this smaller door is a sign which states "Customer Entrance." Both doors are orange in color, while this section of the outside wall is blue. Outside the smaller customer entrance door, and on either side of it, are two concrete posts, painted dark brown, and which stand approximately five feet high and three feet apart. Both posts are approximately 19 inches from the outside wall of the K mart building, and are presumably intended to protect the doorway from damage or interference by backing or parked vehicles. When the customer entrance door is opened, the door will clear the southern post by approximately four inches, but will collide with the northern post. When exiting the customer door, there is a downward step of approximately six inches. There are no windows or transparent panels on or near the customer door which would permit viewing the posts from the interior of the store. At the time plaintiff sustained his injuries the large overhead door was closed.

On October 11, 1985, plaintiff drove to defendant's store and parked near the customer entrance door to the Home Center section of the store. Plaintiff walked past the posts and entered the store through the customer entrance door. Plaintiff testified at trial that he did not recall entering the store through this door prior to the date of his injury, but that it was possible he had. Plaintiff testified that he is a self-employed parking lot designer and striper. He stated that he had done work on the parking lot area of the K mart store at which he was injured, but had done no work in the area of the door at which he incurred his injuries. On direct examination, when asked whether he saw the posts as he entered the store, plaintiff responded, "Yes, sir. I mean they were there. Subconsciously, I guess—they were there when I went out, so, evidently, they were there when I went in." Plaintiff's counsel then asked plaintiff if he had made a mental note of the presence of the posts as he entered the store. Plaintiff responded, "Yes, I guess. I don't know. I mean—they were there. I just don't—." On cross-examination, plaintiff testified as follows concerning his encounter with the posts when he entered the store:

Q: And you noticed these posts when you went inside did you not?
A: Subconsciously.
Q: Well, would it be fair to say that you noticed them more or less, yes?
A: More or less. Yes, sir.
Q: You didn't have trouble getting around those posts on the way in, did you, sir?
A: Not that I recall.

Plaintiff remained in the store for approximately one-half hour, during which time he purchased a large bathroom mirror, which was 5 feet long and approximately 1½ feet wide. The mirror was packed in a cardboard holder, but the face of the mirror was not covered. Plaintiff testified that after he paid for the mirror he left the cash register, carrying the mirror vertically and "kind of to the side." He stated that he did not have the mirror in front of his eyes at that time. When plaintiff reached the door, a store clerk released a security lock, which permitted customers to exit through the door by which plaintiff had entered. Apparently, the door is designed so that customers may freely enter through it during business hours, but as a means of preventing shoplifting, a security lock must be released in order for customers to exit through the door.

Plaintiff opened the door by pressing against it with his left shoulder. Plaintiff estimated that he had taken from a half step to a full step through the door when he "just saw stars, and a—a bad pain, and then saw stars. That was the last I recall." First the mirror, and then plaintiff's head and face, collided with the concrete post. Plaintiff testified that he could not see the post as he exited the store because the mirror blocked his view. He stated he was not in a hurry at the time. Prior to exiting the K mart store, plaintiff was not warned by way of a sign or otherwise of the existence of the posts outside the door.

As a result of the collision, plaintiff sustained a cut to his right cheek. Immediately after the collision, plaintiff could not see out of his right eye. Although part of the vision in that eye has since returned, the center vision in that eye is still obscured. Plaintiff has also experienced severe headaches of a kind which he did not experience before the collision with the post.

A K mart employee who worked in the Home Center department at the time of plaintiff's injuries testified at trial that on any given day, from one to 50 people would use the door through which plaintiff exited. He further testified that he had seen some people brush up against the post, but that prior to October 11, 1985, he had never seen anyone injured as a result of colliding with the post while leaving through the customer entrance door.

At the conclusion of the trial, the jury found for plaintiff and assessed plaintiff's damages at $85,000. The jury further found plaintiff 20% comparatively negligent, resulting in a verdict of $68,000.

The circuit court then granted defendant's motion for judgment notwithstanding the jury's verdict. The circuit court found that it should have allowed defendant's motion for a directed verdict. In entering the judgment n.o.v., the circuit court concluded that defendant had no reason to expect that plaintiff's attention would be distracted when he exited the door or that plaintiff would forget about the posts outside the door. The circuit court further stated that the posts were not inherently dangerous and that they became dangerous only when acted upon by some external force. The court concluded that the only distractions involved in the case were those induced by plaintiff himself. The appellate court affirmed the judgment n.o.v., with one justice dissenting, holding that defendant could not reasonably have been expected to foresee that plaintiff would fail to see or to remember the post, which was an obvious condition and which plaintiff had previously encountered.

Directed verdicts or judgments n.o.v. ought to be entered only in those cases in which all of the evidence, when viewed in its aspect most favorable to the opponent, so overwhelmingly favors movant that no contrary verdict based on that evidence could ever stand. The essential elements of a cause of action based on common law negligence may be stated briefly as follows: the existence of a duty owed by the defendant to the plaintiff, a breach of that duty, and an injury proximately caused by that breach. The sole inquiry before us concerns the existence of a duty, i.e., whether defendant and plaintiff stood in such a relationship to one another that the law imposed upon defendant an obligation of reasonable conduct for the benefit of plaintiff. Whether a duty exists in a particular case is a question of law to be determined by the court. . . .

With respect to conditions on land, the scope of the landowner's or occupier's duty owed to entrants upon his premises traditionally turned on the status of the entrant. The operator of a business, though not an insurer of his customer's safety, owed his invitees a duty to exercise reasonable care to maintain his premises in a reasonably safe condition for use by the invitees. . . . Plaintiff in this case was a business invitee on defendant's premises at the time he was injured. We note that in 1984 the General Assembly enacted the Premises Liability Act (Ill. Rev. Stat. 1987, ch. 80, par. 301 et seq.), which provides, in pertinent part:

§2. The distinction under the common law between invitees and licensees as to the duty owed by an owner or occupier of any premises to such entrants is abolished.

"The duty owed to such entrants is that of reasonable care under the circumstances regarding the state of the premises or acts done or omitted on them." (Ill. Rev. Stat. 1987, ch. 80, par. 302.)

In conjunction with the common law rule governing a landowner's or occupier's duty to invitees there developed a principle that the owner or occupier is not liable to entrants on his premises for harm caused by a condition on the premises of which the entrant is aware or which is obvious. . . . A defendant was thus generally held to have no duty to warn his invitees of, or otherwise protect them from, known or obviously dangerous conditions on his premises. But clearly, in this State, as in others, the "known or obvious risk" principle was sometimes treated as a type of contributory negligence or assumption of the risk.

Prior to this court's adoption of a comparative negligence formula in Alvis v. Ribar (1981), 85 Ill. 2d 1, 52 Ill. Dec. 23, 421 N.E.2d 886 (since modified by Ill. Rev. Stat. 1987, ch. 110, ¶2-1116), it made little difference whether the principle was treated as one of "no duty" or one of contributory negligence. Under either characterization the result was the same: no recovery. In the present case, however, plaintiff argues that the principle that an owner or occupier of land may have no duty to warn or otherwise take reasonable steps to protect those lawfully on his premises of certain conditions on his premises because those conditions are known to the entrant or are open and obvious is incompatible with our system of comparative fault. Plaintiff asserts that the fact a condition causing the injury may be open and obvious, or may have been previously encountered by the plaintiff, is but a factor to be considered in determining the plaintiff's comparative fault.

We agree with plaintiff that the fact a person's injury resulted from his encountering a known or open and obvious condition on a defendant's premises is a proper factor to be considered in assessing the person's comparative negligence. It is unquestionably relevant to whether the injured party was exercising a reasonable degree of care for his own safety. And in this respect a plaintiff's own fault in encountering such a condition will not necessarily bar his recovery. As discussed below, however, we find that the obviousness of a condition is also relevant to the existence of a duty on the part of defendant.

Initially we reject plaintiff's argument that the adoption of comparative negligence in this State has affected the basic duty a landowner or occupier owes to entrants upon his land with respect to such conditions. Some courts and commentators have apparently embraced the position taken by plaintiff in this respect. (See, e.g., Cox v. J.C. Penney Co. (Mo. 1987), 741 S.W.2d 28, 30; Parker v. Highland Park, Inc. (Tex. 1978), 565 S.W.2d 512, 517-18. See also Note, Torts-Assumption of Risk and the Obvious Danger Rule. Primary or Secondary Assumption of Risk?, 18 Land & Water L. Rev. 373, 384-85 (1983).) The primary justification for this approach is the proposition that a consequence of the adoption of comparative negligence is the elimination of those common law devices which act as absolute bars to recovery. We find this argument unpersuasive.

In Dunn v. Baltimore & Ohio R.R. Co. (1989), 127 Ill. 2d 350, 130 Ill. Dec. 409, 537 N.E.2d 738, this court followed the common law rule that a train stopped at a crossing is generally adequate notice and warning of its presence to any traveler who is in the exercise of ordinary care for his own safety, and that the railroad is under no duty to give additional signs, signals or warnings. This court there rejected the plaintiff's argument that the rule, serving as an absolute bar to plaintiff's recovery, is incompatible with comparative negligence principles. We held that "the adoption of comparative negligence does not expand or otherwise alter the duty owed by a railroad to motorists approaching a standing train at a crossing." (127 Ill. 2d at 365, 130 Ill. Dec. 409, 537 N.E.2d 738). . . . Plaintiff here argues that the rationale for our holding in *Dunn* should be limited to the context of railroad crossing cases or that *Dunn* should be overruled. We disagree. In *Dunn,* we recognized that the advent of comparative negligence did not affect the basic duty a defendant owes a plaintiff in negligence cases. . . . We continue to adhere to this principle. Comparative negligence has indeed altered the nature of defenses available to a defendant. (See, e.g., Coney v. J.L.G. Industries, Inc. (1983), 97 Ill. 2d 104, 119 (defenses of misuse and assumption of the risk in strict products liability cases no longer serve as absolute bars to a plaintiff's recovery).) In the present case, however, we are not so much concerned with the defenses available to defendant, but rather with the existence of a duty on the part of defendant in the first instance. . . .

The crux of the issue before us then is whether defendant's general duty of reasonable care extended to the risk encountered by plaintiff. This court has not recently had occasion to address the validity of the "known" or "obvious" risk principle. We do so now. We conclude that to the extent that the rule may have held that the duty of reasonable care owed by an owner or occupier to those lawfully on his premises does not under any circumstances extend to conditions which are known or obvious to such entrants, that rule is not the law in this State.

The traditional rule, endorsed by the original Restatement of Torts, sections 340 and 343 (1934), that an owner or occupier of land has no duty under any circumstances to protect entrants from conditions on his land of which the entrant knows and realizes the risk or which are obvious, has fallen under harsh criticism. Professor Fleming James argued that this rule is "wrong in policy." James, Tort Liability of Occupiers of Land: Duties Owed to Licensees and Invitees, 63 Yale L.J. 605, 628 (1954), *reprinted in* 5 F. Harper, F. James & O. Gray, The Law of Torts §27.13, at 250-51 (2d ed. 1986). . . .

It must be remembered that under our Premises Liability Act, and at least nominally under the common law, the landowner's or occupier's duty toward his invitees is always that of reasonable care. The only sound explanation for the "open and obvious" rule must be either that the defendant in the exercise of reasonable care would not anticipate that the plaintiff would fail to notice the condition, appreciate the risk, and avoid it (see Keeton, Personal Injuries Resulting from Open and Obvious Conditions, 100 U. Pa. L. Rev. 629, 642-43 (1952)), or perhaps that reasonable care under the circumstances would not remove the risk of injury in spite of foreseeable consequences to the plaintiff. But neither of these explanations justifies a per se rule that under no circumstances does the defendant's duty of reasonable care extend to conditions which may be labeled "open and obvious" or of which the plaintiff is in some general sense "aware." Professor Page Keeton noted that "there is perhaps no condition the danger of which is so obvious that all customers under all circumstances would necessarily see and realize the danger in the absence of contributory negligence, and this is particularly true if the further principle so often repeated is accepted that the customer or business invitee is entitled to assume that the premises are reasonably safe for his use." (Keeton, Personal Injuries Resulting from Open and Obvious Conditions, 100 U. Pa. L. Rev. 629, 642 (1952).) Attempting to dispose of litigation by merely invoking such relative and imprecise characterizations as "known" or "obvious" is certainly no adequate substitute for assessing the scope of the defendant's duty under the circumstances in accordance with the considerations previously identified by this court.

Certainly a condition may be so blatantly obvious and in such position on the defendant's premises that he could not reasonably be expected to anticipate that people will fail to protect themselves from any danger posed by the condition. Even in the case of children on the premises, this court has held that the owner or possessor has no duty to remedy conditions presenting obvious risks which children would generally be expected to appreciate and avoid. (Cope v. Doe (1984), 102 Ill. 2d 278, 286, 80 Ill. Dec. 40, 464 N.E.2d 1023 (seven-year-old fell through ice on artificial retention pond); see also Sampson v. Zimmerman (1986), 151 Ill. App. 3d 396, 104 Ill. Dec. 349, 502 N.E.2d 846 (four-year-old burned by candle flame).) Professor James observed that "[i]f people who are likely to encounter a condition may be expected to take perfectly good care of themselves without further precautions, then the condition is not unreasonably dangerous because the likelihood of harm is slight." James, Tort Liability of Occupiers of Land: Duties Owed to Licensees and Invitees, 63 Yale L.J. 605, 623 (1954), *reprinted in* 5 F. Harper, F. James & O. Gray, The Law of Torts §27.13, at 242 (2d ed. 1986).

This is not, as plaintiff here suggests, a resurrection of contributory negligence. The scope of defendant's duty is not defined by reference to plaintiff's negligence or lack thereof. The focus must be on defendant. A major concern is whether defendant could reasonably have foreseen injury to plaintiff. . . .

Turning to the specific facts of the present case, we agree with defendant and the trial court that there is nothing inherently dangerous about the post. It is just an ordinary post. The proper question, however, is not whether the post was inherently dangerous, but whether, under the facts of this case, it was unreasonably dangerous. This question generally cannot be answered by merely viewing the condition in the abstract, wholly apart from the circumstances in which it existed. There may be many conditions on a person's premises which are in fact dangerous, but not "unreasonably" so for any of a number of reasons. For example, as discussed above, the defendant may have no reason to anticipate that an entrant on his premises will fail to see and appreciate the danger. But there may also be conditions which, though seemingly innocuous enough in themselves, indeed present an unreasonable danger under certain circumstances. For example, it may be said that there is ordinarily no unreasonable danger in an ordinary flight of stairs, but stairs may indeed be unreasonably dangerous if, under the circumstances of a particular case, the defendant in the exercise of reasonable care should anticipate that the plaintiff will fail to see them.

This is not to say that the defendant must anticipate negligence on the part of the plaintiff. Generally a party need not anticipate the negligence of others. The inquiry is whether the defendant should reasonably anticipate injury to those entrants on his premises who are generally exercising reasonable care for their own safety, but who may reasonably be expected to be distracted, as when carrying large bundles, or forgetful of the condition after having momentarily encountered it. If in fact the entrant was also guilty of negligence contributing to his injury, then that is a proper consideration under comparative negligence principles.

We agree with the appellate court in the present case that the post with which plaintiff collided is not a hidden danger. Indeed plaintiff walked past the post when entering the store and admitted he was at least "subconsciously" aware of its presence. We disagree with the appellate court's holding, however, that "defendant could not reasonably have been expected to foresee that one of its customers would block his vision with an object which he had purchased and fail to see a five-foot-tall concrete post located outside of an entrance to its store." (185 Ill. App. 3d at 163, 133 Ill. Dec. 170, 540 N.E.2d 1036.) We may well have arrived at a different conclusion if the post would have been located further away from the entrance of the building, or if the plaintiff would not have been carrying any vision-obscuring bundle. . . .

[On these facts, however,] it was reasonably foreseeable that a customer would collide with the post while exiting defendant's store carrying merchandise which could obscure view of the post. Defendant invited customers to use the door through which plaintiff entered and exited, and many customers did use it. Defendant had reason to anticipate that customers shopping in the store would, even in the exercise of reasonable care, momentarily forget the presence of the posts which they may have previously encountered by entering through the customer entrance door. It was also reasonably foreseeable that a customer carrying a large item which he had purchased in the store might be distracted and fail to see the post upon exiting through the door. It should be remembered that the post was located immediately outside the entrance to the Home Center section of defendant's store. Defendant had every reason to expect that customers would carry large, bulky items through that door, particularly where, as here, the large overhead door was closed. The burden on the defendant of protecting against this danger would be slight. A simple warning or a relocation of the post may have sufficed. It is also relevant that there were no windows or transparent panels on the customer entrance doors to permit viewing of the posts from the interior of the store. Indeed defendant's clerk testified that he had seen people brush up against the post while exiting the store. . . .

Our holding does not impose on defendant the impossible burden of rendering its premises injury-proof. Defendant can still expect that its customers will exercise reasonable care for their own safety. We merely recognize that there may be certain conditions which, although they may be loosely characterized as "known" or "obvious" to customers, may not in themselves satisfy defendant's duty of reasonable care. If the defendant may reasonably be expected to anticipate that even those customers in the general exercise of ordinary care will fail to avoid the risk because they are distracted or momentarily forgetful, then his duty may extend to the risk posed by the condition. Whether in fact the condition itself served as adequate notice of its presence or whether additional precautions were required to satisfy the defendant's duty are questions properly left to the trier of fact. The trier of fact may also consider whether the plaintiff was in fact guilty of negligence contributing in whole or in part to his injury, and adjust the verdict accordingly.

In sum we hold that defendant's duty of reasonable care encompassed the risk that one of its customers, while carrying a large, bulky item, would collide with the post upon exiting through the customer door. The jury instructions, which are not challenged by either party, adequately informed the jury of defendant's duty of reasonable care. There was ample evidence presented at trial to support a finding that defendant breached its duty and that the breach proximately caused plaintiff's injury. There was further ample evidence of plaintiff's own negligence contributing to his injury. We, therefore, see no reason to disturb the jury's verdict. The judgments of the circuit and appellate courts are reversed, and this cause is remanded to the circuit court of Champaign County with directions to enter judgment for plaintiff in the amount of $68,000.

Judgments reversed; cause remanded with directions.

E.   Limitations on Liability

1.   The Absence of a General Duty to Rescue

Page 494.   At end of page, add the following text:

An attempt to "constitutionalize" the duty to rescue failed in DeShaney v. Winnebago County Department of Social Services, 489 U.S. 189, 109 S. Ct. 998, 103 L. Ed. 2d 189 (1989). Suit was brought on behalf of a young child who had been severely beaten by his father. The complaint alleged a violation of 42 U.S.C. §1983 (see Section E of Chapter 11 in casebook) by the county Department of Social Services based on its failure to take active steps to protect the plaintiff after it became aware of the father's abusive treatment. The court ruled that the Fourteenth Amendment to the U.S. Constitution, which §1983 is designed to implement, does not require affirmative action by the state to protect the physical well-being of its citizens.

Page 503.   After Tarasoff v. Regents of the University of California, add the following new case:

Diaz Reyes v. United States
770 F. Supp. 58 (D.P.R. 1991)

[The plaintiffs are the surviving wife and children of a person who died of AIDS as a result, they alleged, of AIDS-infected blood given the decedent in a transfusion. Included in the wife's complaint was a count alleging that the decedent's doctor knew that the decedent had tested positive for AIDS but did not tell her. She alleged that she and her husband continued to have conjugal relations, and that although she did not at the time of the complaint test positive, she suffered anxiety that she would at some time test positive and contract AIDS. Reproduced here is that portion of the opinion dealing with this count.]

FUSTE, District Judge . . . Plaintiff Diaz Reyes alleges that the defendant had an independent duty to inform her of her husband's condition. This would presumably have meant that even if he did not want to share the information with his wife, the hospital had a duty to inform her independently. This claim, of course, raises several problems. The first is whether a medical caretaker has any duty whatsoever to inform non-patients of the condition of a patient. Second is the question as to whether a medical caretaker has the right to disregard the privacy interests of the patient and through doing so violate the doctor-patient confidentiality. Our independent review of Puerto Rico law convinces us that, while the issue has not been specifically addressed in this jurisdiction, the Puerto Rico courts would not be prepared to recognize a duty of a doctor to violate the doctor/patient relationship, even to disclose the presence of AIDS to a spouse. The Puerto Rico Legislature has required doctors to report AIDS-positive tests to the Department of Health, but has never required or allowed that a doctor report AIDS to a spouse over the patient's objection. Puerto Rico evidence law recognizes a strong doctor/ patient privilege. Although the Supreme Court of Puerto Rico does require disclosure in some cases before a tribunal, it has never fashioned a court-made rule requiring disclosure of medical conditions to third parties. As a federal court sitting in diversity, we are not free to blaze new paths in local tort law, and we will not do so here. We note that on the federal level, recent Veterans Administration requirements allow for disclosure to a spouse, but only after certain conditions have been met. The new regulations do not require such disclosure. Were we to create a Puerto Rico disclosure duty which is broader than the federal statutory rule (if the Puerto Rico rule required absolute full non-discretionary disclosure to the spouse with no conditions precedent, for instance), thereby creating a tort law duty to disclose where the federal rule precludes disclosure, there might well be a Supremacy clause or preemption problem. Since we hold that Puerto Rico law does not recognize a duty to disclose to family members, we need not reach the Supremacy/preemption issue.

2.   Proximate Cause

a.   Liability Limited to Foreseeable Consequences

(1)   Foreseeable Results

Page 526.   *Before* Marshall v. Nugent, *add the following new cases:*

Lear Siegler, Inc. v. Perez
819 S.W.2d 470 (Tex. 1991)

GAMMAGE, Justice. In this personal injury action, we consider whether a fact issue was raised as to causation in a summary judgment proceeding. The trial court granted summary judgment in part on grounds that, as a matter of law, no causal connection existed between the product manu-factured by Lear Siegler, Inc. and the injury. The court of appeals reversed and remanded, holding plaintiffs' evidence raised a fact issue that pre-cluded summary judgment. Under the particular facts before us, we conclude that causation was negated as a matter of law. Accordingly, we reverse the judgment of the court of appeals and affirm the trial court's judgment.

Rafael Perez, while working for the Texas Highway Department, drove a truck pulling a flashing arrow sign behind a sweeping operation on Highway 83. The function of the sign, which was manufactured by Lear Siegler, was to warn traffic of the highway maintenance. Perez had stopped his vehicle on the traveled portion of the road when a vehicle approached. A van driven by Alfonso Lerma, who had fallen asleep at the wheel, struck the sign, which in turn struck Perez and knocked him through the air to the pavement several yards away. Perez sustained severe injuries from which he subsequently died. Plaintiffs, who are Perez's survivors and legal representatives of his estate, sued the manufacturer on negli-gence and product liability theories. Lear Siegler moved for summary judgment on grounds that the sign, as a matter of law, did not cause the accident. In support of its motion, Lear Siegler offered an uncontradicted affidavit of an eyewitness to the accident stating that the sign was working properly when Lerma's vehicle and other traffic approached.

Plaintiffs, on the other hand, asserted that Perez stopped his truck because the sign malfunctioned, and the defect in the sign thereby placed Perez in the "zone of danger" of Lerma's oncoming vehicle. They sub-mitted a co-employee's affidavit stating that the same warning sign had malfunctioned when he pulled it the day before the accident. The affidavit further stated that, because the wire connections from the sign to the generator worked loose in bumpy driving, it was necessary to get out of the truck and push the wire connections back together. Plaintiffs thus contended that the sign malfunctioned on the day of the accident, that the malfunction was the reason Perez stopped his truck and positioned himself near the sign, and that the eyewitness saw the sign working shortly before the accident because Perez had pushed the wires back or otherwise corrected the malfunction. . . .

Negligent conduct is a cause of harm to another if, in a natural and continuous sequence, it produces an event, and without the negligent conduct such event would not have occurred. There may be more than one proximate cause of an event.

Though we have not adopted the Restatement (Second) of Torts in its entirety in Texas, we find its discussion of "legal cause" instructive:

> In order to be a legal cause of another's harm, it is not enough that the harm would not have occurred had the actor not been negligent. . . .

[T]his is necessary, but it is not of itself sufficient. The negligence must also be a substantial factor in bringing about the plaintiff's harm. The word "substantial" is used to denote the fact that the defendant's conduct has such an effect in producing the harm as to lead reasonable men to regard it as a cause, using that word in the popular sense, in which there always lurks the idea of responsibility, rather than in the so-called "philosophic sense," which includes every one of the great number of events without which any happening would not have occurred. Each of these events is a cause in the so-called "philosophic sense," yet the effect of many of them is so insignificant that no ordinary mind would think of them as causes.

Restatement (Second) of Torts §431, comment a (1965).

We recognize there may be cases in which a product defect or a defendant's negligence exposes another to an increased risk of harm by placing him in a particular place at a given time. Nonetheless, there are certain situations in which the happenstance of place and time is too attenuated from the defendant's conduct for liability to be imposed.

It is undisputed that Lerma was asleep, and proper operation of the flashing arrow sign would have had no effect on his conduct. Plaintiffs assert that, had the sign functioned properly, Perez would not have been at the place where the collision occurred at the time it occurred. We conclude that these particular circumstances are too remotely connected with Lear Siegler's conduct to constitute legal cause. If Perez had instead taken the sign back to the highway department office where the roof caved in on him, we likewise would not regard it as a legal cause.

The trial court correctly held the defect, whether under a products liability or negligence theory of recovery, was not a legal cause of the accident and resulting injuries and death. We reverse the judgment of the court of appeals and affirm the trial court's summary judgment that plaintiffs take nothing against Lear Siegler.

Mitchell v. Gonzales
54 Cal. 3d 1041, 819 P.2d 872, 1 Cal. Rptr. 2d 913 (1991)

Lucas, Chief Justice. In this case we decide whether BAJI No. 3.75, the so-called proximate cause instruction, which contains a "but for" test of cause in fact, should continue to be given in this state, or whether it should be disapproved in favor of BAJI No. 3.76, the so-called legal cause instruction, which employs the "substantial factor" test of cause in fact.[132a]

132a. BAJI No. 3.75, requested by defendants and given by the trial court, provides: "A proximate cause of [injury] [damage] [loss] [or] [harm] is a cause which, in natural and

I. Facts

[The plaintiff's 12-year-old son, Damechie, drowned in a boating accident, and the plaintiff sued the defendants for wrongful death alleging that the defendants were negligent in supervising the decedent.]

The jury, by special verdict, concluded that defendants were negligent but that the negligence was not a cause of the death. . . .

The trial court denied plaintiff's motions for a new trial or a judgment notwithstanding the verdict. The Court of Appeals reversed.

II. Discussion

As explained below, we conclude the Court of Appeal correctly determined that the trial court prejudicially erred when it refused BAJI No. 3.76 and instead gave BAJI No. 3.75. Our discussion proceeds in two steps. We begin by determining whether instructional error occurred. Our analysis focuses on whether conceptual and grammatical flaws in BAJI No. 3.75 may confuse jurors and lead them to improperly limit their findings on causation, and whether BAJI No. 3.76 is a superior alternative instruction. Because we find error, we next analyze prejudice and conclude that there is a reasonable probability that BAJI No. 3.75 misled the jurors into finding that defendants' negligence was not a "proximate cause" of Damechie's death and that a result more favorable to plaintiffs would have occurred if the jury had been instructed under BAJI No. 3.76. Accordingly, we affirm the Court of Appeal's decision reversing the judgment of the trial court.

A. Alleged Instructional Error

As Dean Prosser observed over 40 years ago, "Proximate cause remains a tangle and a jungle, a palace of mirrors and a maze. . . ." Cases "indicate that 'proximate cause' covers a multitude of sins, that it is a complex term of highly uncertain meaning under which other rules,

---

continuous sequence, produces the [injury] [damage] [loss] [or] [harm] and without which the [injury] [damage] [loss] [or] [harm] would not have occurred." Because of the "without which" language, courts often refer to this instruction as the "but for" instruction of causation. BAJI No. 3.76, requested by plaintiffs and refused by the trial court, provides: "A legal cause of [injury] [damage] [loss] [or] [harm] is a cause which is a substantial factor in bringing about the [injury] [damage] [loss] [or] [harm]." We emphasize that despite the use of the terms *proximate cause* and *legal cause*, BAJI Nos. 3.75 and 3.76 are instructions on cause in fact. Issues that are properly referred to as questions of proximate or legal cause are contained in other instructions. (See, e.g., BAJI No. 3.79 [superseding causes].)

doctrines and reasons lie buried. . . ." (Prosser, Proximate Cause in California (1950) 38 Cal. L. Rev. 369, 375.)

One of the concepts included in the term *proximate cause* is *cause in fact,* also referred to as *actual cause.* Indeed, for purposes of BAJI No. 3.75, "so far as a jury is concerned 'proximate cause' *only* relates to causation in fact." (Com. to BAJI No. 3.75, italics added.) "There are two widely recognized tests for establishing cause in fact. The 'but for' or 'sine qua non' rule, unfortunately labeled 'proximate cause' in BAJI No. 3.75, asks whether the injury would not have occurred but for the defendant's conduct. The other test, labeled 'legal cause' in BAJI No. 3.76, asks whether the defendant's conduct was a substantial factor in bringing about the injury."

BAJI Nos. 3.75 and 3.76 are *alternative* instructions that should not jointly be given in a single lawsuit. . . . It has generally been recognized that the "but for" test contained in BAJI No. 3.75 should not be used when two "causes concur to bring about an event and either one of them operating alone could have been sufficient to cause the result. In those few situations, where there are concurrent [independent] causes, our law provides one cannot escape responsibility for his negligence on the ground that identical harm would have occurred without it. The proper rule for such situations is that the defendant's conduct is a cause of the event because it is a material element and a substantial factor in bringing it about." Vecchione v. Carlin (1980) 111 Cal. App. 3d 351, 168 Cal. Rptr. 571. . . .

This case presents the issue of whether BAJI No. 3.75 should be given in any negligence action. . . .

The misunderstanding engendered by the term "proximate cause" has been documented. In a scholarly study of 14 jury instructions, BAJI No. 3.75 produced proportionally the most misunderstanding among laypersons. (Charrow, Making Legal Language Understandable: A Psycholinguistic Study of Jury Instructions (1979) 79 Colum. L. Rev. 1306, 1353 (hereafter Psycholinguistic Study).) The study noted two significant problems with BAJI No. 3.75. First, because the phrase "natural and continuous sequence" precedes "the verb it is intended to modify, the construction leaves the listener with the impression that the cause itself is in a natural and continuous sequence. Inasmuch as a single 'cause' cannot be in a continuous sequence, the listener is befuddled." (Psycholinguistic Study, supra, 79 Colum. L. Rev. at p. 1323.) Second, in one experiment, "the term 'proximate cause' was misunderstood by 23% of the subjects. . . . They interpreted it as 'approximate cause,' 'estimated cause,' or some fabrication." (Id., at p. 1353.)

Our Courts of Appeal have recognized the serious problems with the language of BAJI No. 3.75. In Fraijo v. Hartland Hospital [(1979)] 99

Cal. App. 3d 331, 160 Cal. Rptr. 246, the court criticized the instruction because it appeared to place an undue emphasis on "nearness." Nonetheless, "despite the criticism of the 'but for' language in BAJI No. 3.75, the most recent edition of California Jury Instructions (Civil) [citation omitted] . . . allow[s] the trial judge to exercise a discretion in selecting his preference between . . . the 'proximate cause' instruction found in BAJI No. 3.75, or the 'legal cause' instruction found in BAJI No. 3.76." ([*Fraijo*], at p. 346, 160 Cal. Rptr. 246.)

The *Fraijo* court said, "We agree that BAJI No. 3.75—the proximate cause instruction—is far from constituting a model of clarity in informing a jury as to what is meant by proximate causation. . . . Nevertheless, in view of its long history of being considered a correct statement of the law by the courts of this state, we are not inclined to hold that BAJI No. 3.75 is an erroneous instruction. Although we believe such a determination should be made, we consider that the determination ought to be made by our Supreme Court and not by an intermediate reviewing court." (Fraijo v. Hartland Hospital, supra, 99 Cal. App. 3d 331, 347, 160 Cal. Rptr. 246; see also Maupin v. Widling [(1987)] 192 Cal. App. 3d 568, 574, 237 Cal. Rptr. 521 ("BAJI No. 3.75 is famous for causing juror confusion. It has been criticized for its inexact terminology and incorrect sentence structure."); John B. Gunn Law Corp. v. Maynard (1987) 189 Cal. App. 3d 1565, 1571, 235 Cal. Rptr. 180 (instruction misleading, but "it has never been held error in California to instruct in terms of BAJI No. 3.75 due to lack of intelligibility.").)

We believe the foregoing authorities properly criticize BAJI No. 3.75 for being conceptually and grammatically deficient. The deficiencies may mislead jurors, causing them, if they can glean the instruction's meaning despite the grammatical flaws, to focus improperly on the cause that is spatially or temporally closest to the harm.

In contrast, the "substantial factor" test, incorporated in BAJI No. 3.76 and developed by the Restatement Second of Torts, section 431 (com. to BAJI No. 3.76) has been comparatively free of criticism and has even received praise. "As an instruction submitting the question of causation in fact to the jury in intelligible form, it appears impossible to improve on the Restatement's 'substantial factor [test.]' " (Prosser, Proximate Cause in California, supra, 38 Cal. L. Rev. 369, 421.) It is "sufficiently intelligible to any layman to furnish an adequate guide to the jury, and it is neither possible nor desirable to reduce it to lower terms." (Id., at p. 379.)

Moreover, the "substantial factor" test subsumes the "but for" test. "If the conduct which is claimed to have caused the injury had nothing at all to do with the injuries, it could not be said that the conduct was a factor, let alone a substantial factor, in the production of the injuries."

(Doupnik v. General Motors Corp. (1990) 225 Cal. App. 3d 849, 861, 275 Cal. Rptr. 715.)

Not only does the substantial factor instruction assist in the resolution of the problem of independent causes, as noted above, but "[i]t aids in the disposition . . . of two other types of situations which have proved troublesome. One is that where a similar, but not identical result would have followed without the defendant's act; the other where one defendant has made a clearly proved but quite insignificant contribution to the result, as where he throws a lighted match into a forest fire. But in the great majority of cases, *it produces the same legal conclusion as the but-for test.* Except in the classes of cases indicated, no case has been found where the defendant's act could be called a substantial factor when the event would have occurred without it; nor will cases very often arise where it would not be such a factor when it was so indispensable a cause that without it the result would not have followed." (Prosser & Keeton on Torts, supra, §41, at pp. 267-268, fns. omitted, italics added.). . . .

We recognize that BAJI No. 3.76 is not perfectly phrased. The term "legal cause" may be confusing. As part of the psycholinguistic study referred to above, the experimenters rewrote BAJI No. 3.75 to include the term "legal cause." The study found that "25% of the subjects who heard 'legal cause' misinterpreted it as the opposite of an 'illegal cause.' We would therefore recommend that the term 'legal cause' not be used in jury instructions; instead, the simple term 'cause' should be used, with the explanation that the law defines 'cause' in its own particular way." (Psycholinguistic Study, supra, 79 Colum. L. Rev. at p. 1353.). . . .

The continued use of BAJI No. 3.75 as an instruction on cause in fact is unwise. The foregoing amply demonstrates that BAJI No. 3.75 is grammatically confusing and conceptually misleading. Continued use of this instruction will likely cause needless appellate litigation regarding the propriety of the instructions in particular cases. Use of BAJI No. 3.76 will avoid much of the confusion inherent in BAJI No. 3.75. It is intelligible and easily applied. We therefore conclude that BAJI No. 3.75, the so-called proximate cause instruction, should be disapproved and that the court erred when it refused to give BAJI No. 3.76 and instead gave BAJI No. 3.75.

B. Prejudicial Effect of Erroneous Instruction

Having determined it was error to refuse to give BAJI No. 3.76 and instead give BAJI No. 3.75, we must decide whether the error was so prejudicial as to require reversal.

[We] analyze the closeness of the jury's verdict. The jury found on [votes of 9 to 3 and 11 to 1 that the various defendants] were negligent (i.e., they breached a duty of care to [decedent].) Yet the jury [by votes of 12 to 0 and 10 to 2 found that the negligence of the various defendants was not a cause of the death.]

The verdict as to causation was not particularly close. It seems that the jury did follow BAJI No. 3.75 but was misled by the instruction's flaws: Having found the defendants negligent, it is illogical and inconsistent on this record to conclude that they were not a cause in fact of Damechie's death. Accordingly, we conclude it is reasonably probable that the jury was confused by BAJI No. 3.75 and overemphasized the "but for" nature of the instruction. . . .

Based on the foregoing analysis, we conclude that it is reasonably probable a result more favorable to the plaintiffs would have resulted if BAJI No. 3.75 had not been given.

Conclusion

We conclude that BAJI No. 3.75 should be disapproved, that the trial court erred when it gave the instruction, and that such error was prejudicial. Accordingly, the decision of the Court of Appeal reversing the judgment in favor of defendants is affirmed.

[The dissenting opinion of KENNARD, Associate Justice, is omitted.]

3. Special Instances of Nonliability for Foreseeable Consequences

a. Mental and Emotional Harm

Page 580.   *Before* Dillon v. Legg, *add the following text:*

In Mauro v. Raymark Industries, Inc., supplement p. 25, the court ruled that the plaintiff could recover emotional harm damages stemming from his fear that he would at some time in the future contract cancer. Persons alleging emotional harm from fear of future injury have brought suit in a variety of other contexts. In Rossi v. Almaraz, 1991 WL 166924 (Md. Cir. Ct. 1991), and Burk v. Sage, 747 F. Supp. 285 (E.D. Pa. 1990), for example, the plaintiffs' actions for emotional harm were based on fear of contracting AIDS. In *Rossi,* the plaintiff was a patient of a surgeon who died of AIDS shortly after operating on the plaintiff. The plaintiff's test was negative, and the court ruled that there could be no recovery for the emotional harm absent proof that the plaintiff had been exposed to the AIDS virus. There was no proof that the operation was such that would result in exposure. In *Sage,* the plaintiff was pricked with a needle that was available to treat AIDS patients, but he could not prove that the needle had actually come into contact with such a patient. The plaintiff, like the plaintiff in *Rossi,* tested negative, and the court refused to permit damages for the fear of contracting AIDS in the future.

Another context that has stimulated considerable litigation involves heart valves. In Brinkman v. Shiley, Inc., 732 F. Supp. 33 (M.D. Pa. 1988), the plaintiff, a wearer of a mechanical heart valve manufactured by the defendant, alleged that he saw a television program detailing the defectiveness of some heart valves of the sort used by the plaintiff and manufactured by the defendant. The valve had not malfunctioned at the time of the suit, but the plaintiff was concerned that it might do so in the future. The court, however, ruled that there could be no recovery. In Kahn v. Shiley, Inc., 217 Cal. App. 3d 848, 266 Cal. Rptr. 106 (1990), the court ruled that the plaintiff could not recover for "heart valve anxiety" in a tort-based products liability suit, but could recover on proof of fraud. The manufacturer of the heart valves agreed conditionally to set up a $205 million fund to compensate the 55,000 persons with functioning valves who may fear a future malfunction. The settlement does not affect the suits filed on behalf of the 310 persons who died as a result of valve malfunction. See 20 Prod. Safety & Liab. Rep. (BNA) 117 (1992).

Similar suits may be brought by women who have received silicone breast implants, in light of the stories about the problems many of these women have had. See, e.g., Hilts, Maker Is Depicted as Fighting Tests on Implant Safety, N.Y. Times, Jan. 13, 1992, col. 6, at 1 (N.E.). At least one such suit has already been brought. See 20 Prod. Safety & Liab. Rep. (BNA) 117 (1992).

Page 593.   Before Johnson v. State, *add the following new case:*

Thing v. La Chusa
48 Cal. 3d 644, 771 P.2d 814, 257 Cal. Rptr. 865 (1991)

EAGLESON, Justice. The narrow issue presented by the parties in this case is whether the Court of Appeal correctly held that a mother who did not witness an accident in which an automobile struck and injured her child may recover damages from the negligent driver for the emotional distress she suffered when she arrived at the accident scene. The more important question this issue poses for the court, however, is whether the "guidelines" enunciated by this court in Dillon v. Legg (1968) 68 Cal. 2d 728, 69 Cal. Rptr. 72, 441 P.2d 912, are adequate, or if they should be refined to create greater certainty in this area of the law.

Although terms of convenience identify the cause of action here as one for negligent infliction of emotional distress (NIED) and the plaintiff as a "bystander" rather than a "direct victim," the common law tort giving rise to plaintiffs' claim is negligence. . . . It is in that context that we consider the appropriate application of the concept of "duty" in an area that has long divided this court—recognition of the right of persons, whose only injury is emotional distress, to recover damages when that distress is caused by knowledge of the injury to a third person caused by the defendant's negligence. Although we again find ourselves divided, we shall resolve some of the uncertainty over the parameters of the NIED action, uncertainty that has troubled lower courts, litigants, and, of course, insurers.

Upon doing so, we shall conclude that the societal benefits of certainty in the law, as well as traditional concepts of tort law, dictate limitation of bystander recovery of damages for emotional distress. In the absence of physical injury or impact to the plaintiff himself, damages for emotional distress should be recoverable only if the plaintiff: (1) is closely related to the injury victim; (2) is present at the scene of the injury-producing event at the time it occurs and is then aware that it is causing injury to the victim and, (3) as a result suffers emotional distress beyond that which would be anticipated in a disinterested witness.

I

[The plaintiff's son was injured in an automobile accident that the plaintiff did not witness. She was near the scene, and, on being informed of the accident, she "rushed to the scene where she saw her bloody and unconscious child, whom she believed was dead, lying in the roadway." She brought suit against the defendants for emotional harm she suffered as a result of witnessing her son in his injured condition. The trial judge granted the defendants' motion for summary judgment, which was reversed by the Court of Appeal.]

III   Limitations in Negligence Actions

[The court surveyed the law preceding Dillon v. Legg, including Amaya v. Home Ice, Fuel & Supply Co., 59 Cal. 3d 295, 379 P.2d 513, 29 Cal. Rptr. 33 (1963).]

The *Amaya* view was short lived, however. Only five years later, the

77

decision was overruled in Dillon v. Legg, supra, 68 Cal. 2d 728, 69 Cal. Rptr. 72, 441 P.2d 912. In the ensuing 20 years, like the pebble cast into the pond, *Dillon*'s progeny have created ever widening circles of liability. Post-*Dillon* decisions have now permitted plaintiffs who suffer emotional distress, but no resultant physical injury, and who were not at the scene of and thus did not witness the event that injured another, to recover damages on grounds that a duty was owed to them solely because it was foreseeable that they would suffer that distress on learning of injury to a close relative. . . .

The difficulty in defining the limits on recovery anticipated by the *Amaya* court was rejected as a basis for denying recovery, but the court did recognize that "to limit the otherwise potentially infinite liability which would follow every negligent act, the law of torts holds defendant amenable only for injuries to others which to defendant at the time were reasonably foreseeable." (*Dillon,* supra, 68 Cal. 2d at p. 739, 69 Cal. Rptr. 72, 441 P.2d 912.) Thus, while the court indicated that foreseeability of the injury was to be the primary consideration in finding duty, it simultaneously recognized that policy considerations mandated that infinite liability be avoided by restrictions that would somehow narrow the class of potential plaintiffs. But the test limiting liability was itself amorphous. . . .

The *Dillon* court anticipated and accepted uncertainty in the short term in application of its holding, but was confident that the boundaries of this NIED action could be drawn in future cases. In sum, as former Justice Potter Stewart once suggested with reference to that undefinable category of materials that are obscene, the *Dillon* court was satisfied that trial and appellate courts would be able to determine the existence of a duty because the court would know it when it saw it. (See Jacobellis v. Ohio (1964) 378 U.S. 184, 197, 84 S. Ct. 1676, 1683, 12 L. Ed. 2d 793 (conc. opn. of Stewart, J.).) Underscoring the questionable validity of that assumption, however, was the obvious and unaddressed problem that the injured party, the negligent tortfeasor, their insurers, and their attorneys had no means short of suit by which to determine if a duty such as to impose liability for damages would be found in cases other than those that were "on all fours" with *Dillon*. Thus, the only thing that was foreseeable from the *Dillon* decision was the uncertainty that continues to this time as to the parameters of the third-party NIED action.

IV *Post-*Dillon *Extension*

The expectation of the *Dillon* majority that the parameters of the tort would be further defined in future cases has not been fulfilled. Instead, subsequent decisions of the Courts of Appeal and this court, have created more uncertainty. And, just as the "zone of danger" limitation was abandoned in *Dillon* as an arbitrary restriction on recovery, the *Dillon* guidelines have been relaxed on grounds that they, too, created arbitrary limitations on recovery. Little consideration has been given in post-*Dillon* decisions to the importance of avoiding the limitless exposure to liability that the pure foreseeability test of "duty" would create and towards which these decisions have moved.

[The court's discussion of the post-*Dillon* California cases is omitted.]

V   Clarification of the Right to Recover for NIED

Not surprisingly, this "case-to-case" or ad hoc approach to development of the law that misled the Court of Appeal in this case has not only produced inconsistent rulings in the lower courts, but has provoked considerable critical comment by scholars who attempt to reconcile the cases. . . .

Our own prior decisions identify factors that will appropriately circumscribe the right to damages, but do not deny recovery to plaintiffs whose emotional injury is real even if not accompanied by out-of-pocket expense. Notwithstanding the broad language in some of those decisions, it is clear that foreseeability of the injury alone is not a useful "guideline" or a meaningful restriction on the scope of the NIED action. . . . It is apparent that reliance on foreseeability of injury alone in finding a duty, and thus a right to recover, is not adequate when the damages sought are for an intangible injury. In order to avoid limitless liability out of all proportion to the degree of a defendant's negligence, and against which it is impossible to insure without imposing unacceptable costs on those among whom the risk is spread, the right to recover for negligently caused emotional distress must be limited.

[The court's discussion of the *Dillon* factor involving the relationship of the plaintiff to the primary victim is omitted. The court discussed a variety of contexts in which that issue can arise, including claims for loss of consortium (see Borer v. American Airlines, casebook p.598) and for wrongful life (see Turpin v. Sortini, casebook p.620).]

Similar reasoning justifies limiting recovery to persons closely related by blood or marriage since, in common experience, it is more likely that they will suffer a greater degree of emotional distress than a disinterested witness to negligently caused pain and suffering or death. Such limitations are indisputably arbitrary since it is foreseeable that in some cases unrelated persons have a relationship to the victim or are so affected by the traumatic event that they suffer equivalent emotional distress. As we have observed, however, drawing arbitrary lines is unavoidable if we are to limit liability and establish meaningful rules for application by litigants and lower courts.

No policy supports extension of the right to recover for NIED to a larger class of plaintiffs. Emotional distress is an intangible condition experienced by most persons, even absent negligence, at some time during their lives. Close relatives suffer serious, even debilitating, emotional reactions to the injury, death, serious illness, and evident suffering of loved ones. These reactions occur regardless of the cause of the loved one's illness, injury, or death. That relatives will have severe emotional distress is an unavoidable aspect of the "human condition." The emotional distress for which monetary damages may be recovered, however, ought not to be that form of acute emotional distress or the transient emotional reaction to the occasional gruesome or horrible incident to which every person may potentially be exposed in an industrial and sometimes violent society. Regardless of the depth of feeling or the resultant physical or mental illness that results from witnessing violent events, persons unrelated to those injured or killed may not now recover for such emotional upheaval even if negligently caused. Close relatives who witness the accidental injury or death of a loved one and suffer emotional trauma may not recover when the loved one's conduct was the cause of that emotional trauma. The overwhelming majority of "emotional distress" which we endure, therefore, is not compensable.

Unlike an award of damages for intentionally caused emotional distress which is punitive, the award for NIED simply reflects society's belief that a negligent actor bears some responsibility for the effect of his conduct on persons other than those who suffer physical injury. In identifying those persons and the circumstances in which the defendant will be held to redress the injury, it is appropriate to restrict recovery to those persons who will suffer an emotional impact beyond the impact that can be anticipated whenever one learns that a relative is injured, or dies, or the emotion felt by a "disinterested" witness. The class of potential plaintiffs should be limited to those who because of their relationship suffer the greatest emotional distress. When the right to recover is limited in this manner, the liability bears a reasonable relationship to the culpability of the negligent defendant.

The elements which justify and simultaneously limit an award of damages for emotional distress caused by awareness of the negligent infliction of injury to a close relative are those noted in Ochoa [v. Superior Court, 39 Cal. 3d 159, 703 P.2d 1, 216 Cal. Rptr. 661 (1985)]—the traumatic emotional effect on the plaintiff who contemporaneously observes both the event or conduct that causes serious injury to a close relative and the injury itself. Even if it is "foreseeable" that persons other than closely related percipient witnesses may suffer emotional distress, this fact does not justify the imposition of what threatens to become unlimited liability for emotional distress on a defendant whose conduct is simply negligent. Nor does such abstract "foreseeability" warrant continued reliance on the assumption that the limits of liability will become any clearer if lower courts are permitted to continue approaching the issue on a "case-to-case" basis some 20 years after *Dillon.*

We conclude, therefore, that a plaintiff may recover damages for emotional distress caused by observing the negligently inflicted injury of a third person if, but only if, said plaintiff: (1) is closely related to the injury victim; (2) is present at the scene of the injury producing event at the time it occurs and is then aware that it is causing injury to the victim; and (3) as a result suffers serious emotional distress—a reaction beyond that which would be anticipated in a disinterested witness and which is not an abnormal response to the circumstances. These factors were present in *Ochoa* and each of this court's prior decisions upholding recovery for NIED.

The dictum in *Ochoa* suggesting that the factors noted in the *Dillon* guidelines are not essential in determining whether a plaintiff is a foreseeable victim of defendant's negligence should not be relied on. The merely negligent actor does not owe a duty the law will recognize to make monetary amends to all persons who may have suffered emotional distress on viewing or learning about the injurious consequences of his conduct. . . . Experience has shown that, contrary to the expectation of the *Dillon* majority, and with apology to Bernard Witkin, there are clear judicial days on which a court can foresee forever and thus determine liability but none on which that foresight alone provides a socially and judicially acceptable limit on recovery of damages for that injury.

VI Disposition

The undisputed facts establish that plaintiff was not present at the scene of the accident in which her son was injured. She did not observe defendant's conduct and was not aware that her son was being injured. She could not, therefore, establish a right to recover for the emotional distress she suffered when she subsequently learned of the accident and observed its consequences. The order granting summary judgment was proper.

The judgment of the Court of Appeal is reversed.

KAUFMAN, Justice, concurring.

We granted review in this case because of the obvious and continuing difficulties that have plagued trial courts and litigants in the area of negligent infliction of emotional distress. Of course, any meaningful review of the issue necessarily entails reappraising, in the light of 20 years of experience, our landmark holding in Dillon v. Legg (1968) 68 Cal. 2d 728, 69 Cal. Rptr. 72, 441 P.2d 912, that a plaintiff may recover for the emotional distress induced by the apprehension of negligently caused injury to a third person. Two such "reappraisals" have now been suggested.

The majority opinion by Justice Eagleson proposes to convert *Dillon*'s flexible "guidelines" for determining whether the risk of emotional injury was foreseeable or within the defendant's duty of care, into strict "elements" necessary to recovery. While conceding that such a doctrinaire approach will necessarily lead to "arbitrary" results, Justice Eagleson nevertheless concludes that "[g]reater certainty and a more reasonable limit on the exposure to liability for negligent conduct" require strict limitations. (Maj. opn., p. 879 of 257 Cal. Rptr., p. 828 of 771 P.2d.)

Justice Broussard, in dissent [reprinted below], opposes the effort to rigidify the *Dillon* guidelines. He urges, instead, that the court remain faithful to the guidelines as originally conceived—as specific but "flexible" limitations on liability—and adhere to *Dillon*'s original reliance on "foreseeability as a general limit on tort liability." (Dis. opn. of Broussard, J., p. 868 of 257 Cal. Rptr., p. 817 of 771 P.2d.) Justice Broussard denies that *Dillon* has failed to afford adequate guidance to the lower courts or to confine liability within reasonable limits. On the contrary, the *Dillon* approach, in the dissent's view, has provided—and continues to provide— a workable and "*principled* basis for determining liability. . . ." (Id., at p. 895 of 257 Cal. Rptr., at p. 844 of 771 P.2d, italics added.)

With all due respect, I do not believe that either the majority opinion or the dissent has articulated a genuinely "principled" rule of law. On the one hand, experience has shown that rigid doctrinal limitations on bystander liability, such as that suggested by Justice Eagleson, result inevitably in disparate treatment of plaintiffs in substantially the same position. To be sure, the majority freely—one might say almost cheerfully—acknowledges that its position is arbitrary; yet nowhere does it consider the cost of such institutionalized caprice, not only to the individuals involved, but to the integrity of the judiciary as a whole.

On the other hand, two decades of adjudication under the inexact guidelines created by *Dillon* and touted by the dissent, has, if anything, created a body of case law marked by even greater confusion and inconsistency of result.

The situation, therefore, calls for a wholesale reappraisal of the wisdom of permitting recovery for emotional distress resulting from injury to others.

[The courts discussion of earlier California cases and cases from other states rejecting *Dillon* is omitted.]

While the courts rejecting bystander liability have cited a number of reasons, one argument in particular has been considered dispositive: *Dillon*'s confident prediction that future courts would be able to fix just and sensible boundaries on bystander liability has been found to be wholly illusory—both in theory and in practice. . . .

Twenty-five years ago, this court posed a series of rhetorical questions concerning the guidelines later adopted in *Dillon:* "[H]ow soon is 'fairly contemporaneous?' What is the magic in the plaintiff's being 'present'? Is the shock any less immediate if the mother does not know of the accident until the injured child is brought home? And what if the plaintiff is present at the scene but is nevertheless unaware of the danger or injury to the third person until shortly after the accident has occurred . . . ?" (Amaya v. Home Ice, Fuel & Supply Co., supra, 59 Cal. 2d at p. 313, 29 Cal. Rptr. 33, 379 P.2d 513.) As the foregoing sampling of *Dillon*'s progeny vividly demonstrates, we are no closer to answers today than we were then. The questions, however, are no longer hypothetical—they are real: Is there any rational basis to infer that Mrs. Arauz was any less traumatized than Mrs. Dillon because she saw her bloody infant five minutes after it was struck by defendant's car? Was the Hathaways' suffering mitigated by the fact that they witnessed their child literally in death's throes, but failed to witness the precipitating event? Could it be argued that the emotional distress is even more traumatic, more foreseeable, for parents such as the Hathaways who fail to witness the accident and later blame themselves for allowing it to occur?

Clearly, to apply the *Dillon* guidelines strictly and deny recovery for emotional distress because the plaintiff was not a contemporaneous eyewitness of the accident but viewed the immediate consequences, ill serves the policy of compensating foreseeable victims of emotional trauma. Yet once it is admitted that temporal and spatial limitations bear no rational relationship to the likelihood of psychic injury, it becomes impossible to define, as the *Amaya* court well understood, any "sensible or just stopping point." (59 Cal. 2d at p. 311, 29 Cal. Rptr. 33, 379 P.2d 513.) By what humane and principled standard might a court decide, as a matter of law, that witnessing the bloody and chaotic aftermath of an accident involving a loved one is compensable if viewed within 1 minute of impact but noncompensable after 15? or 30? Is the shock of standing by while others undertake frantic efforts to save the life of one's child any less real or foreseeable when it occurs in an ambulance or emergency room rather than at the "scene"?

Obviously, a "flexible" construction of the *Dillon* guidelines cannot, ultimately, avoid drawing arbitrary and irrational distinctions any more than a strict construction. Justice Burke was right when he observed of the *Dillon* guidelines, "Upon analysis, their seeming certainty evaporates into arbitrariness, and inexplicable distinctions appear." (Dillon v. Legg, supra, 68 Cal. 2d at p. 749, 69 Cal. Rptr. 72, 441 P.2d 912, dis. opn. of Burke, J.)

C.   *Dillon*'s Arbitrary Approach Should Be Overturned

Of course, it could be argued that recovery—not rationality—is the essential thing; that ultimately justice is better served by arbitrarily denying recovery to some, than by absolutely denying recovery to all. I find this argument to be unpersuasive, however, for two reasons.

First, the cost of the institutionalized caprice which *Dillon* has wrought should not be underestimated. The foremost duty of the courts in a free society is the principled declaration of public norms. The legitimacy, prestige and effectiveness of the judiciary—the "least dangerous branch"— ultimately depend on public confidence in our unwavering commitment to this ideal. Any breakdown in principled decisionmaking, any rule for which no principled basis can be found and clearly articulated, subverts and discredits the institution as a whole.

It is not always easy, of course, to accommodate the desire for individual justice with the need for reasoned, well-grounded, general principles. We sacrifice the latter for the sake of the former, however, only at our peril. For the "power-base" of the courts, as noted above, is rather fragile; it consists of the perception of our role in the structure of American government as the voice of reason, and the faith that the laws we make today, we ourselves will be bound by tomorrow. Any "rule"—such as *Dillon*'s—which permits and even encourages judgments based not on universal standards but individual expediency, erodes the public trust which we serve, and on which we ultimately depend.

There is a second reason, apart from the inherently corrosive effect of arbitrary rules, that points to the conclusion that "bystander" liability should not be retained. The interest in freedom from emotional distress caused by negligent injury to a third party is simply not, in my view, an interest which the law can or should protect. It is not that the interest is less than compelling. The suffering of a parent from the death or injury of a child is terribly poignant, and has always been so. It is the very universality of such injury, however, which renders it inherently unsuitable to legal protection. . . .

A final argument against overruling *Dillon* is, of course, the simple fact that it has been the law for 20 years. Stare decisis should not be lightly dismissed in any thoughtful reconsideration of the law. History and experience, however, are the final judge of whether a decision was right or wrong, whether it should be retained, modified or abandoned. In this case, history and experience have shown, as the *Amaya* court accurately predicted, that the quest for sensible and just limits on bystander liability is "an inherently fruitless one." (59 Cal. 2d at p. 313, 29 Cal. Rptr. 33, 379 P.2d 513.)

Adherence to precedent cannot justify the perpetuation of a policy ill-conceived in theory and unfair in practice. As Justice Harlan aptly observed: "[A] judicious reconsideration of precedent cannot be as threatening to public faith in the judiciary as continued adherence to a rule unjustified in reason, which produces different results for breaches of duty in situations that cannot be differentiated in policy. . . ." (Moragne v. States Marine Lines, Inc. (1970) 398 U.S. 375, 405, 90 S. Ct. 1772, 1790, 26 L. Ed. 2d 339.)

For the foregoing reasons, therefore, I would overrule Dillon v. Legg, supra, 68 Cal. 2d 728, 69 Cal. Rptr. 72, 441 P.2d 912, and reinstate Amaya v. Home Ice, Fuel & Supply Co., supra, 59 Cal. 2d 295, 29 Cal. Rptr. 33, 379 P.2d 513 as the law of this state. Since the plaintiff was indisputably not within the zone of danger and could not assert a claim for emotional distress as the result of fear for her own safety, she could not establish a right to recover. Accordingly, I concur in the majority's conclusion that the order granting summary judgment in this case was proper.

[The dissenting opinion of MOSK, J., is omitted.]

BROUSSARD, Justice, dissenting.

I dissent. . . .

The majority grope for a "bright line" rule for negligent infliction of emotional distress actions, only to grasp an admittedly arbitrary line which will deny recovery to victims whose injuries from the negligent acts of others are very real. In so doing, the majority reveal a myopic reading of Dillon v. Legg, supra, 68 Cal. 2d 728, 69 Cal. Rptr. 72, 441 P.2d 912. They impose a strict requirement that plaintiff be present at the scene of the injury-producing event at the time it occurs and is aware that it is causing injury to the victim. This strict requirement rigidifies what *Dillon* forcefully told us should be a flexible rule, and will lead to arbitrary results. I would follow the mandate of *Dillon* and maintain that foreseeability and duty determine liability, with a view toward a policy favoring reasonable limitations on liability. There is no reason why these general rules of tort law should not apply to negligent infliction of emotional distress actions. . . .

Page 598.   Before Problem 27, add the following new case:

Marlene F. v. Affiliated Psychiatric Medical Clinic, Inc.

48 Cal. 3d 583, 770 P.2d 278, 257 Cal. Rptr. 98 (1989)

ARGUELLES, Justice. Can the mother of a minor child state a claim for the negligent infliction of emotional distress against the psychotherapist who, consulted to treat both mother and son, sexually molested the boy? As, in the circumstances of this case, the therapist's conduct breached a duty of care owed [the mother] as well as her child, we hold she can.

Facts

In the summer of 1980, the mothers of minor children Robert F., Phillip G., and Eric R. brought their sons to the Affiliated Psychiatric Medical Clinic, Inc., to obtain counseling for family emotional problems. The clinic assigned all three children to one of its employees, the same psychologist in each case, who began treating the mothers as well because he believed each child's psychological problems arose in part from difficulties in the relationship between mother and son.

In the spring of 1982, the boys' mothers discovered that the therapist had sexually molested their sons by fondling the boys' genitals and that he had engaged in other lewd conduct with the children. Each child was molested at the clinic offices, and Robert was also molested elsewhere.

The mothers confronted the owner and the clinical director of the clinic with this information. They were told that the therapist had done nothing "illegal" but that he would no longer be assigned minor patients. The therapist later wrote a letter of "explanation" to the parents, in which he stated he would no longer treat minor patients and would himself undergo psychotherapy.

The mothers of Robert and Phillip brought suit against the clinic, its owner, its clinical director, and the treating therapist for negligent infliction of emotional distress, alleging that the molestation of their sons had caused them serious mental and emotional suffering and further disruption of their family relationships. . . .

All defendants successfully demurred to this cause of action. The Court of Appeal affirmed, acknowledging that the mothers had suffered from the mistreatment of their children but reasoning that they failed to state a claim under either the "bystander witness" theory of Dillon v. Legg

(1968) 68 Cal. 2d 728, 69 Cal. Rptr. 72, 441 P.2d 912 or the "direct victim" theory of Molien v. Kaiser Foundation Hospitals (1980) 27 Cal. 3d 916, 167 Cal. Rptr. 831, 616 P.2d 813, because they were neither present at the time the torts were committed nor the actual targets of the therapist's unprofessional conduct. We granted review to determine whether the mothers of Robert and Phillip, although neither bystander witnesses nor the immediate objects of the tortious conduct, could state claims for the negligent infliction of emotional distress.

Discussion . . .

In Dillon v. Legg, supra, 68 Cal. 2d 728, 69 Cal. Rptr. 72, 441 P.2d 912, we held that a mother could recover from a negligent motorist for the emotional distress she suffered from witnessing the accident that caused the death of her child. Recognizing that foreseeability of the injury was but the threshold element in determining the existence of a duty of care, we identified a number of factors designed to limit the scope of the duty to "exclud[e] the remote and unexpected" and to specify the class of potential plaintiffs entitled to recover for the emotional distress occasioned by witnessing the injury of another. (Id. at pp. 740-741, 69 Cal. Rptr. 72, 441 P.2d 912.) In Molien v. Kaiser Foundation Hospitals, supra, 27 Cal. 3d 916, 167 Cal. Rptr. 831, 616 P.2d 813, we held that a husband could recover from his wife's doctor for the emotional distress he suffered from the misdiagnosis of his wife as having syphilis and the advice that he be physically examined as well. Reasoning that the husband was a "direct victim" of the tort in view of the nature of the doctor's conduct, we held that defendants owed him a duty of care. (Id. at p. 923, 167 Cal. Rptr. 831, 616 P.2d 813.)

As in Dillon v. Legg, supra, 68 Cal. 2d 728, 69 Cal. Rptr. 72, 441 P. 2d 912, we stressed certain inherently limiting factors, in particular that the doctor instructed the wife to tell her husband of the diagnosis and to advise him to be examined as well, and that the doctor's error was singularly likely to result in marital discord and in emotional distress to the husband. "Because the disease is normally transmitted only by sexual relations, it is rational to anticipate that both husband and wife would experience anxiety, suspicion, and hostility when confronted with what they had every reason to believe was reliable medical evidence of a particularly noxious infidelity. We thus agree with plaintiff that the alleged tortious conduct of [the doctor] was directed to him as well as to his wife." (Molien v. Kaiser Foundation Hospitals, supra, 27 Cal. 3d at p. 923, 167 Cal. Rptr. 831, 616 P.2d 813.)

Our decision did not, however, purport to create a cause of action for the negligent infliction of emotional distress based solely upon the foreseeability that serious emotional distress might result. It is plainly foreseeable, for example, that close family members of a patient would suffer severe emotional distress if told the patient had been diagnosed as suffering from a terminal illness, but without more, the patient's physician would not be liable for that distress whether or not the diagnosis was erroneous. Damages for severe emotional distress, rather, are recoverable in a negligence action when they result from the breach of a duty owed the plaintiff that is assumed by the defendant or imposed on the defendant as a matter of law, or that arises out of a relationship between the two. Our decision in Molien v. Kaiser Foundation Hospitals, supra, 27 Cal. 3d 916, 167 Cal. Rptr. 831, 616 P.2d 813, acknowledged this, and permitted recovery for the emotional distress suffered by the husband when his wife's doctor not only erroneously diagnosed the wife as suffering from a sexually transmitted disease but affirmatively acted to have that misdiagnosis communicated to her husband. By directing the husband be told of a diagnosis that foreseeably would disrupt the marital relationship and require the husband to be physically examined, the doctor assumed a duty to convey accurate information and the husband accordingly was a "direct victim" of the doctor's negligence.

In the present case, the complaint explicitly and expressly alleged that the mothers of Robert and Phillip, as well as the children, were patients of the therapist; specifically, that he "undertook to treat both [mother and son] for their intra-family difficulties by providing psychotherapy to both. . . ." It further alleged that the therapist "was aware of the relationship between the patients" and that he "believed that one of the problems in the family arose from the relationship between [mother and son]." In other words, the counselling was not directed simply at each mother and son as individuals, but to both in the context of the family relationship. And the complaint alleged that the discovery by the mothers of the therapist's sexual misconduct caused them serious emotional distress, further disrupting that family relationship.

In these circumstances, the therapist, as a professional psychologist, clearly knew or should have known in each case that his sexual molestation of the child would directly injure and cause severe emotional distress to his other patient, the mother, as well as to the parent-child relationship that was also under his care. His abuse of the therapeutic relationship and molestation of the boys breached his duty of care to the mothers as well as to the children. . . .

It bears repeating that the mothers here were the patients of the therapist along with their sons, and the therapist's tortious conduct was accordingly directed against both. They sought treatment for their children—as they had the right, and perhaps even the obligation, to do—

and agreed to be treated themselves to further the purposes of the therapy. They were plainly entitled to recover for the emotional distress they suffered.

Conclusion

We conclude that the mothers stated a cause of action for the negligent infliction of emotional distress against the therapist who molested their sons in the course of a professional relationship involving both mother and son.

[Arguelles, J., also wrote an opinion concurring, not surprisingly, in the opinion he wrote for the court. In his concurring opinion, he urged that the plaintiffs had stated a cause of action for intentional infliction of emotional harm.]

b. Injury to Personal Relationships

Page 598.   Before Borer v. American Airlines, Inc., add the following new case:

Feliciano v. Rosemar Silver Co.
401 Mass. 141, 514 N.E.2d 1095 (1987)

O'CONNOR, Justice. Marcial Feliciano and the plaintiff Dolores Feliciano commenced an action in the Superior Court against Miguel Costa and Rosemar Silver Company (Rosemar) claiming that Marcial sustained personal injuries and the plaintiff sustained loss of consortium due to Costa's wrongful conduct in the course of his employment by Rosemar. Rosemar moved for summary judgment on the loss of consortium claim. That motion was allowed, and the plaintiff appealed. . . . We now affirm the judgment.

According to the plaintiff's deposition and affidavit submitted in connection with Rosemar's summary judgment motion, Marcial and the plaintiff had lived together as husband and wife for approximately twenty years before Marcial's injuries in 1981 "as a de facto married couple," although they were not legally married until 1983. During those years, the plaintiff used Marcial's surname, and the plaintiff and Marcial held themselves out as husband and wife, had joint savings accounts, filed joint tax returns, jointly owned their home, depended on each other for companionship, comfort, love and guidance, and maintained a sexual relationship to the exclusion of all others. The question on appeal is whether, in those circumstances, the plaintiff may recover for loss of consortium. We answer that question in the negative.

"Marriage is not merely a contract between the parties. It is the foundation of the family. It is a social institution of the highest importance. The Commonwealth has a deep interest that its integrity is not jeopardized." French v. McAnarney, 290 Mass. 544, 546, 195 N.E. 714 (1935). Our recognition of a right of recovery for the loss of a spouse's consortium, see Diaz v. Eli Lilly & Co., 364 Mass. 153, 302 N.E.2d 555 (1973), promotes that value. Conversely, that value would be subverted by our recognition of a right to recover for loss of consortium by a person who has not accepted the correlative responsibilities of marriage. This we are unwilling to do.

Furthermore, as a matter of policy, it must be recognized that tort liability cannot be extended without limit. Distinguishing between the marriage relationship and the myriad relationships that may exist between mere cohabitants serves the purpose of limiting protection to interests and values that are reasonably ascertainable. That cohabitants must have a "stable and significant" relationship to qualify for loss of consortium recovery, a standard relied on in the case of Butcher v. Superior Court of Orange County, 139 Cal. App. 3d 58, 70, 188 Cal. Rptr. 503 (1983), is an unsatisfactorily vague and indefinite standard.

We are not aware that any State court of last resort has recognized a right of recovery for loss of consortium outside of marriage. The two Federal decisions cited by the plaintiff interpreting State law as allowing such recovery, Sutherland v. Auch Inter-Borough Transit Co., 366 F. Supp. 127 (E.D. Pa. 1973), and Bulloch v. United States, 487 F. Supp. 1078 (D.N.J. 1980), were subsequently repudiated in the relevant States. See Leonardis v. Morton Chem. Co., 184 N.J. Super. 10, 445 A.2d 45 (1982); Childers v. Shannon, 183 N.J. Super. 591, 444 A.2d 1141 (1982); Rockwell v. Liston, 71 Pa. D. & C.2d 756 (1975).

Judgment affirmed.

c. Prenatal Harm

(2)   Actions on Behalf of Children for Their Own Harm

Page 620.   Before Turpin v. Sortini, *add the following new case:*

Stallman v. Youngquist
125 Ill. 2d 267, 531 N.E.2d 355 (1988)

Justice CUNNINGHAM delivered the opinion of the court:
Plaintiff, Lindsay Stallman, brought suit by her father and next friend, Mark Stallman, against defendant Bari Stallman and codefendant Clarence Youngquist (not a party to this appeal) for prenatal injuries allegedly sustained by plaintiff during an automobile collision between Bari Stallman's automobile and the automobile driven by Clarence Youngquist. Defendant Bari Stallman is the mother of plaintiff. Defendant was approximately five months pregnant with plaintiff and was on her way to a restaurant when the collision occurred.
 . . . There are two issues on appeal: the status of the parental immunity doctrine in Illinois and the tort liability of mothers to their children for the unintentional infliction of prenatal injuries. For the reasons developed below, this court does not recognize a cause of action brought by or on behalf of a fetus, subsequently born alive, against its mother for the unintentional infliction of prenatal injuries. This decision requires us to hold that the circuit court was correct when it granted defendant's motion for summary judgment. Therefore, it is unnecessary for this court to reach the issue concerning the status of the parental immunity doctrine.

Case Background

 . . . Count II of plaintiff's second amended complaint, the subject matter of this appeal, charged defendant with negligence, the direct and proximate result of which caused the fetus (the unborn plaintiff) to be thrown about in the womb of her mother (defendant) resulting in serious and permanent injury to plaintiff.
 . . . [T]he circuit court granted the defendant's motion for summary judgment. Plaintiff appealed this decision to the appellate court. . . .
 The . . . court reversed the order of the circuit court granting the summary judgment and remanded the cause to permit the parties to proceed to trial on the merits. . . . We granted this appeal. [The court did not adequately address] the preliminary issue whether a cause of

action by or on behalf of a fetus, subsequently born alive, may be asserted
against its mother for the unintentional infliction of prenatal injuries. This
court holds that such a cause of action shall not be recognized.

This holding makes unnecessary the consideration of the issue of the
parental immunity doctrine. . . .

Prenatal Negligence

The issue whether a cause of action exists by or on behalf of a fetus,
subsequently born alive, against its mother for the unintentional infliction
of prenatal injuries is an issue of first impression in this court. We begin
with a review of the area of tort liability for prenatal negligence as it has
developed in regards to third persons.

It was not until 1884, in Dietrich v. Northampton (1884), 138 Mass.
14, that such a case came before a court in the United States alleging a
cause of action for prenatal injuries. In *Dietrich,* Judge Oliver Wendell
Holmes held that the common law did not recognize a cause of action in
tort for prenatal injuries to a fetus. Judge Holmes denied that such an
action may lie primarily because the fetus "was a part of the mother at
the time of the injury, [and] any damage to it which was not too remote
to be recovered for at all was recoverable by her." (138 Mass. at 17.)
After *Dietrich* and until 1946, all courts in the United States which
considered the question agreed: no action would lie for injuries sustained
by a fetus which became apparent on its birth.

This court was one of the first to consider the question of the liability
of third persons for prenatal negligence after the *Dietrich* case. In Allaire
v. St. Luke's Hospital (1900), 184 Ill. 359, 56 N.E. 638, it was held that
no action would lie for injuries to a fetus, only days away from birth,
due to the negligence of the defendant hospital where the mother of the
plaintiff was a patient awaiting the delivery of the plaintiff. In *Allaire,*
this court affirmed the opinion of the appellate court, which had stated,
" 'That a child before birth is, in fact, a part of the mother and is only
severed from her at birth, cannot, we think, be successfully disputed.' "
(184 Ill. at 368, 56 N.E. 638.) This court adopted the reasoning of the
appellate court that the plaintiff, at the time of the injury, did not have
a distinct and independent existence from his mother; the injury was to
the mother and not to the plaintiff. 184 Ill. at 365, 56 N.E. 638.

Allaire is primarily remembered today for the dissent of Mr. Justice
Boggs, who asked the question: "Should compensation for his injuries be
denied on a mere theory, known to be false, that the injury was not to
his [or her] person but to the person of the mother?" 184 Ill. at 374, 56
N.E. 638 (Boggs, J., dissenting).

The rule recognizing the right to bring an action for injuries inflicted on a fetus by a person not its mother is as pervasive and established now as was the contrary rule before 1946. This court overruled *Allaire* in Amann v. Faidy (1953), 415 Ill. 422, 114 N.E.2d 412, and recognized a cause of action under the wrongful death statute for the death of an infant who, while in a viable condition, sustained a prenatal injury due to the negligence of a third person. Later, in Rodriguez v. Patti (1953), 415 Ill. 496, 114 N.E.2d 721, this court recognized a common law right of action for personal injuries to an infant, a viable fetus, when wrongfully injured due to the negligence of third persons. Much later, in Chrisafogeorgis v. Brandenberg (1973), 55 Ill. 2d 368, 304 N.E.2d 88, this court held that a wrongful death action could be maintained on behalf of a stillborn child who sustained injuries due to the negligence of third persons while a viable fetus.

The early reliance by courts on viability as a point at which with certainty it could be said that the fetus and the woman who is the mother of the fetus are two separate entities proved to be troublesome. Most courts have since abandoned viability as a requirement for a child to bring an action for prenatal injuries inflicted by third persons. . . .

In Renslow v. Mennonite Hospital (1977), 67 Ill. 2d 348, 10 Ill. Dec. 484, 367 N.E.2d 1250, this court rejected viability as a requirement in a cause of action for prenatal injuries suffered by a fetus due to the negligence of third persons. . . .

The above case law has grown out of circumstances in which the defendant was a third person and not the mother of the plaintiff. Plaintiff in the instant case asserts that she should be able to bring a cause of action for prenatal injuries against her mother just as she would be able to bring a cause of action for prenatal injuries against a third person. . . .

This court has never been asked to decide if, by becoming pregnant, a woman exposes herself to a future lawsuit by or on behalf of the fetus which will become her child. At one time a fetus was seen as only a part of the woman who was the mother of the child. When someone tortiously injured a pregnant woman and her fetus sustained injury as a result, no legal protection would have been extended to the subsequently born child. Today, when the tortious acts of another towards a woman who is or may become pregnant harms a fetus, there is a legally cognizable cause of action for the injury to both the woman and the subsequently born child.

In the path which some courts have taken on the road which has recognized recovery for a child for injuries inflicted on it as a fetus, there has been an articulation of a "legal right to begin life with a sound mind and body." The articulation of this right to recover against third-person tortfeasors has served to emphasize that it is not just the pregnant woman alone who may be harmed by the tortious act of another but also the fetus, whose injuries become apparent at its birth.

It is clear that the recognition of a legal right to begin life with a sound mind and body on the part of a fetus which is assertable after birth against its mother would have serious ramifications for all women and their families, and for the way in which society views women and women's reproductive abilities. The recognition of such a right by a fetus would necessitate the recognition of a legal duty on the part of the woman who is the mother; a legal duty, as opposed to a moral duty, to effectuate the best prenatal environment possible. The recognition of such a legal duty would create a new tort: a cause of action assertable by a fetus, subsequently born alive, against its mother for the unintentional infliction of prenatal injuries.

It is the firmly held belief of some that a woman should subordinate her right to control her life when she decides to become pregnant or does become pregnant: anything which might possibly harm the developing fetus should be prohibited and all things which might positively affect the developing fetus should be mandated under penalty of law, be it criminal or civil. Since anything which a pregnant woman does or does not do may have an impact, either positive or negative, on her developing fetus, any act or omission on her part could render her liable to her subsequently born child. While such a view is consistent with the recognition of a fetus' having rights which are superior to those of its mother, such is not and cannot be the law of this State.

A legal right of a fetus to begin life with a sound mind and body assertable against a mother would make a pregnant woman the guarantor of the mind and body of her child at birth. A legal duty to guarantee the mental and physical health of another has never before been recognized in law. Any action which negatively impacted on fetal development would be a breach of the pregnant woman's duty to her developing fetus. Mother and child would be legal adversaries from the moment of conception until birth. The error that a fetus cannot be harmed in a legally cognizable way when the woman who is its mother is injured has been corrected; the law will no longer treat the fetus as only a part of its mother. The law will not now make an error of a different sort, one with enormous implications for all women who have been, are, may be, or might become pregnant: the law will not treat a fetus as an entity which is entirely separate from its mother.

. . . It is foreseeable that any act or omission by a pregnant woman could impact on fetal development. . . .

If a legally cognizable duty on the part of mothers were recognized, then a judicially defined standard of conduct would have to be met. It must be asked, By what judicially defined standard would a mother have her every act or omission while pregnant subjected to State scrutiny? By what objective standard could a jury be guided in determining whether a pregnant woman did all that was necessary in order not to breach a legal duty to not interfere with her fetus' separate and independent right to be born whole? In what way would prejudicial and stereotypical beliefs about the reproductive abilities of women be kept from interfering with a jury's determination of whether a particular woman was negligent at any point during her pregnancy?

Holding a third person liable for prenatal injuries furthers the interests of both the mother and the subsequently born child and does not interfere with the defendant's right to control his or her own life. Holding a mother liable for the unintentional infliction of prenatal injuries subjects to State scrutiny all the decisions a woman must make in attempting to carry a pregnancy to term, and infringes on her right to privacy and bodily autonomy. This court has said that "the judiciary will . . . exercise its traditional role of drawing rational distinctions, consonant with current perceptions of justice, between harms which are compensable and those which are not." (Renslow v. Mennonite Hospital, 67 Ill. 2d at 358, 10 Ill. Dec. 484, 367 N.E.2d 1250.) Logic does not demand that a pregnant woman be treated in a court of law as a stranger to her developing fetus.

It would be a legal fiction to treat the fetus as a separate legal person with rights hostile to and assertable against its mother. The relationship between a pregnant woman and her fetus is unlike the relationship between any other plaintiff and defendant. No other plaintiff depends exclusively on any other defendant for everything necessary for life itself. No other defendant must go through biological changes of the most profound type, possibly at the risk of her own life, in order to bring forth an adversary into the world. It is, after all, the whole life of the pregnant woman which impacts on the development of the fetus. As opposed to the third-party defendant, it is the mother's every waking and sleeping moment which, for better or worse, shapes the prenatal environment which forms the world for the developing fetus. That this is so is not a pregnant woman's fault: it is a fact of life.

In practice, the reproduction of our species is necessarily carried out by individual women who become pregnant. No one lives but that he or she was at one time a fetus in the womb of its mother. Pregnancy does not come only to those women who have within their means all that is necessary to effectuate the best possible prenatal environment: any female of child-bearing age may become pregnant. Within this pool of potential defendants are representatives of all socio-economic backgrounds: the well-educated and the ignorant; the rich and the poor; those women who have access to good health care and good prenatal care and those who, for an infinite number of reasons, have not had access to any health care services.

The circumstances in which each individual woman brings forth life are as varied as the circumstances of each woman's life. Whether a standard of care to which a woman would be held while pregnant should vary according to whether a pregnancy was planned or unplanned, to whether a woman knew she was pregnant soon after conception or only knew after several months, to whether she had the financial resources with which to access the best possible medical care available or was unable to get any prenatal care are all questions which deserve much thought and reflection.

There are far-reaching issues of public policy inherent in the question whether to recognize a cause of action in tort for maternal prenatal negligence. Judicial scrutiny into the day-to-day lives of pregnant women would involve an unprecedented intrusion into the privacy and autonomy of the citizens of this State. This court holds that if a legally cognizable duty on the part of pregnant women to their developing fetuses is to be recognized, the decision must come from the legislature only after thorough investigation, study and debate.

. . . In holding that no cause of action will lie for maternal prenatal negligence, this court emphasizes that we in no way minimize the public policy favoring healthy newborns. Pregnant women need access to information about the risks inherent in everyday living on a developing fetus and need access to health care for themselves and their developing fetuses. It is, after all, to a pregnant woman's advantage to do all she can within her knowledge and power to bring a healthy child into this world. The way to effectuate the birth of healthy babies is not, however, through after-the-fact civil liability in tort for individual mothers, but rather through before-the-fact education of all women and families about prenatal development.

A cause of action by a fetus against its mother for the unintentional infliction of prenatal injuries is denied. The cause is remanded . . . for proceedings consistent with this opinion.

Page 630.   Before Problem 28, add the following new case:

Lynch v. Bay Ridge Obstetrical and Gynecological Assoc., P.C.
77 N.Y.2d 632, 532 N.E.2d 1239, 536 N.Y.S.2d 11 (1988)

HANCOCK, Judge. Plaintiffs appeal from an order dismissing their malpractice complaint for failure to state a cause of action. In her complaint . . . plaintiff alleges that she consulted defendant Rubino, her gynecologist, because she had not had a menstrual period for over three months and her "home pregnancy tests" were negative. After a visual examination and with no blood or urine analysis, defendant informed her that she was not pregnant. Without explaining any of the attendant risks, he prescribed the hormonal drug Provera. When plaintiff had the prescription filled, she became aware—from the warning on the label and advice given by the pharmacist—that the drug was known to pose a serious risk of producing congenital defects in the child if ingested during early pregnancy. Relying on Rubino's advice that she was not pregnant, plaintiff took the drug as prescribed. When menstruation did not occur, she consulted another gynecologist who ascertained from laboratory tests that she was indeed pregnant and cautioned her about the drug's potentially harmful effects on a fetus in early stages. Fearing that these harmful effects had occurred, plaintiff and her husband elected to have the pregnancy terminated.

Plaintiff alleges that defendants' negligence forced her either to risk having a congenitally defective child or to submit to an abortion in violation of her "personal, moral and religious convictions." She seeks damages for her physical, psychological, and emotional injuries resulting from the abortion and from having to decide whether to undergo it.

The courts below . . . viewed the case as involving an injury to the fetus for which plaintiffs could not recover emotional or psychological damages. Additionally, the Appellate Division held that Rubino's conduct could not have been the proximate cause of the injuries stemming from the abortion. . . . [T]he court reasoned, plaintiffs here acted "on their own, without the affirmative advice of the defendants, [and] thereupon took the final step of procuring an abortion" (134 A.D.2d 240, 242, 520 N.Y.S.2d 431). We now modify.

The complaint and affidavits sufficiently define a cause of action in malpractice for the physical and emotional injuries suffered by plaintiff as a result of defendants' negligence in rendering medical services to plaintiff, and, thereby, breaching their duty of care owed directly to her.

Contrary to defendants' contentions, plaintiff is not seeking to recover for emotional distress resulting from injuries inflicted on the fetus. . . . The breach of duty claimed by plaintiff is Rubino's failure to perform a pregnancy test before advising her that she was not pregnant and before prescribing a drug with potentially harmful side effects if taken during early pregnancy. Indeed, according to her pleading *she* was the patient and *she* was the one injured by the negligent diagnosis and prescription. It is the erroneous advice that she was not pregnant—not an injury to a third person . . . which plaintiff asserts, led to the actions directly causing her injuries: her ingestion of the dangerous drug and her decision to terminate the pregnancy to avoid the drug's harmful effects. Reduced to its essentials, the case presents a malpractice action based on medical advice which put plaintiff in the position of having to make decisions and take actions which caused her physical and emotional injuries. That these decisions and actions involved an abortion does not, as defendants suggest, require us to regard the case as something it is not—i.e., an effort by plaintiff to assert a claim for damages on behalf of her unborn child for injuries done to it or a claim for damages based on plaintiff's emotional and psychological stress in witnessing and knowing of the injury to the fetus and its loss.

In addressing defendants' contention that the claimed negligence could not, as a matter of law, be the proximate cause of the injuries incident to the abortion, we must, of course, assume the truth of the allegations in the complaint and supporting affidavits. Ordinarily, plaintiff's allegations that the injury was a consequence of her physician's negligent advice would be sufficient to create a question of fact for the jury. Defendants argue, however, that this case presents an exception to the rule because plaintiff did not submit to the abortion on the advice of her physician . . . but made the choice to proceed on her own. The independence of plaintiff's decision, defendants contend, elevates her choice to a superseding cause which absolves them from liability. We disagree.

We have recognized that an intervening act which is "not foreseeable in the normal course of events, or independent of or far removed from the defendant's conduct . . . may well be a superseding act which breaks the causal nexus. . . ." There is, we conclude, a factual question presented here: whether, under the circumstances, it could reasonably be expected that plaintiff, upon discovering that she had taken the drug in the mistaken belief that she was not pregnant, would elect to undergo an abortion.

. . . Applying these rules here and assuming the truth of the allegations in the complaint, it is apparent that plaintiff's "choice" to have an abortion cannot be said to be, as a matter of law, a superseding cause. As the complaint alleges, the physician's negligent diagnosis and treatment were the precipitating causes of all that followed; but for the gynecologist's conduct, plaintiff would not have been in the position of having to choose between two objectionable alternatives: undergo an abortion or risk having a baby with serious birth defects. That plaintiff made the very choice forced upon her by defendants' negligence cannot insulate them from legal responsibility for such conduct.

We conclude, however, that plaintiff's cross motion for partial summary judgment was properly denied. The order of the Appellate Division should be modified, with costs to appellants, by denying defendants' motion to dismiss and, as so modified, affirmed.

TITONE, Judge (dissenting).

Because the majority has not adequately considered the consequences of its present holding, I write separately to express my own dissenting views.

It is elementary that, except in limited circumstances not present here, a person cannot recover for emotional shock sustained as a result of injury to another. This rule has traditionally been applied to prohibit a mother's recovery for the emotional distress she suffered as a result of injury or death to the fetus she carried. Further, the circumstances under which the law permits recovery for purely emotional trauma resulting from a frightening event are extremely limited.

While acknowledging these principles, the majority attempts to treat this case as a garden-variety tort action seeking recovery for the physical, as well as emotional, injuries plaintiff sustained as a result of defendants' alleged malpractice. . . . However, the only physical injuries plaintiff was able to allege were the loss of live fetal tissue and blood, coupled with the pain and discomfort, that attends a normal abortion. I do not, of course, intend to minimize or belittle the physical trauma that accompanies many, if not most, abortions. I emphasize this point only to demonstrate that the "physical injury" on which plaintiff's suit—including its claim for severe emotional and spiritual damages—is based is really nothing more than an ordinary elective abortion similar to that undergone by thousands of women each year. . . .

While I am certainly sympathetic with the suffering of plaintiffs such as Mrs. Lynch and I am as disturbed as the majority by the grossly negligent medical conduct that has been alleged here, I cannot agree that the recognition of such a cause of action is sound, at least in light of the present state of the law. If Mrs. Lynch had decided not to terminate her pregnancy and instead carried the child to term, she might have been rewarded with the birth of a healthy child, in which case there would, of course, be no basis for recovery. . . . Even more to the point, if the feared result had actually occurred and the child had been born deformed, Mrs. Lynch would have had no right to seek recovery for the anguish she would unquestionably feel at seeing her child suffer over its lifetime. In such circumstances, recovery would be denied because it would embroil the court in the impossible calculus involved in weighing the "anguish that only parents can experience upon the birth of a[n afflicted] child" against the "love that even an abnormality cannot fully dampen." In my view, assessing the monetary value of the suffering that Mrs. Lynch experienced, and discounting it in recognition that she found abortion to be a less harrowing option than carrying the pregnancy to term, is an equally difficult—and indeed an impossible— calculation to make.

On an even more fundamental level, I am disturbed by the message that the court sends when it permits Mrs. Lynch to recover while denying relief to similarly situated women who have chosen to carry their pregnancies to term and have borne a deformed or impaired child. A rule affording such a preference to the decision to abort is unquestionably inconsistent with "the 'very nearly uniform high value' which the law and mankind have placed upon human life." The decision to terminate or continue a pregnancy is a matter of private choice with which the courts cannot, and should not, interfere. By rewarding the decision to abort with an opportunity to recover for emotional injury that is specifically withheld from the woman who carries the pregnancy to term, the court has, however unintentionally, embroiled itself in precisely the type of value judgment and line-drawing that it quite properly sought to avoid. . . .

Chapter 8

Products Liability

A. Liability for Manufacturing Flaws

1. The Plaintiff's Prima Facie Case: Bases of Liability

c. Strict Liability in Tort

Page 733. *Before* **Vandermark v. Ford Motor Company,** *add the following:*

Henderson and Twerski, A Proposed Revision of Section 402A of the Restatement (Second) of Torts
Excerpted from 77 Cornell L. Rev. — (1992)

I. Introduction

Only rarely do provisions of the American Law Institute's Restatements of the Law rise to the dignity of holy writ. Even more rarely do individual comments to Restatement sections come to symbolize important, decisive developments that dominate judicial thinking. Nevertheless, section 402A of the Restatement (Second) of Torts is such a provision. Literally thousands upon thousands of products liability decisions in the past twenty-five years have explicitly referred to, and come to grips with, that section.[5a] Among products liability followers one need only identify an issue as presenting "a comment k problem," or identify a legislative proposal as "a comment i provision," to capture instantly the essence of the relevant debate and incorporate nearly thirty years of legal controversy, development and refinement.

5a. In a letter to the authors dated October 11, 1991, Marianne M. Walker, A.L.I. Restatement Case Citations Editor, asserts: "In my nine years with the American Law Institute I have found §402A to be the most frequently cited section of any Restatement." After reviewing more than 700 pages of citations in Appendices and pocket parts, confirmed by a computer-assisted search, we conservatively estimate that no fewer than 3,000 published court opinions have cited §402A to the time of this writing.

Given that section 402A has achieved the status of sacred scripture, our proposal to replace it with new text and new comments may strike some readers as blasphemous. What prompts such audacity? Quite simply, doctrinal developments in products liability have placed such a heavy gloss on the original text of and comments to section 402A as to render them anachronistic and at odds with their currently discerned objectives. By changing the relevant language to conform to current understandings— by restating the Restatement—we hope to clarify much of the confusion that has arisen over the years.

Only recently, while working on this article, we learned that the American Law Institute itself has decided that the products liability sections of the Restatement (Second) of Torts, including section 402A, need revision. Especially in light of this decision, our task of proposing a revision of section 402A must be approached with caution and deliberate care. Language that has been interpreted by so many courts over such a substantial period of time cannot be cavalierly discarded. At the same time, issues that once posed burning questions have now been well settled and new areas of controversy dominate the landscape. We have thus chosen a moderate approach to drafting our suggested revision. We intend to stay as close as possible to shared perceptions of the evolved meanings of the original section and its comments. We do not fancy ourselves as radical reformers, although we express preferences, based on widely recognized normative criteria, when choices are appropriate. Finally, we propose to identify those areas in which true controversy reigns and in which neither predictions nor recommendations are in order.

Rather than indulge in a lengthy introduction detailing the background of section 402A's promulgation in 1963 and its subsequent history to date,[5b] we will (as they say), cut to the chase. With more than a little chutzpah (but not a trace of false modesty), we offer our proposed revision of section 402A of the Restatement of Torts, together with our "Official" comments.

5b. For useful treatments of the background and subsequent history of §402A, see generally William L. Prosser, The Fall of the Citadel (Strict Liability to the Consumer), 50 Minn. L. Rev. 791 (1966); Jay M. Smyser, Products Liability and the American Law Institute: A Petition for Rehearing, 42 U. Det. L.J. 343 (1965); John W. Wade, Strict Tort Liability for Products: Past, Present and Future, 13 Cap. U.L. Rev. 335 (1984).

II.   A Revised Section 402A with Revised Comments

§402A.   Special Liability of One Who Sells a Defective Product

(1) One who sells any product in a defective condition is subject to liability for harm to persons or property proximately caused by the product defect if the seller is engaged in the business of selling such a product.

(2) The rule stated in Subsection (1) applies in the case of a claim based on a

(a) manufacturing defect even though the seller exercised all possible care in the preparation and marketing of the product; or

(b) design defect only if the foreseeable risks of harm presented by the product, when and as marketed, could have been reduced at reasonable cost by the seller's adoption of a safer design; or

(c) warning defect only if the seller failed to provide reasonable instructions or warnings about nonobvious product-related dangers that were known, or should have been known, to the seller.

Comments: . . .

h. Design defects. Courts have created several different tests to establish liability for design defects. A majority of courts use some version of a risk-utility balancing test, either by directly adopting a negligence approach or by adopting some version of the approach set forth in this section. Liability attaches only when the plaintiff proves that the defendant failed to adopt a safer, cost-effective design that would have prevented all or part of the plaintiff's harm. A significant number of courts, however, make recovery dependent on whether the product design fails to meet reasonable consumer expectations. Most of these courts also consider the availability of a reasonable-cost, safer alternative design in deciding whether the defendant's design is acceptable. Admittedly, the formal structure of the liability standard differs somewhat from one court to another. Whether the risk-utility balancing is based on the view of the reasonable consumer or the reasonable product seller is a detail left to the various jurisdictions.

The requirement in subsection (2)(b) that the plaintiff demonstrates that a safer design could have been adopted at reasonable cost introduces an important element of materiality. The alternative design must be sufficiently safer than the actual design to have prevented or substantially reduced the harm for which the plaintiff seeks recovery. Thus, in almost every case, the plaintiff must do more than merely show that the defendant's design could have been made "just a little safer."

At bottom, the "reasonable-cost, safer design" approach discussed in this section is that taken by a majority of American courts. A few courts have adopted idiosyncratic tests for design defect. For example, one state court applies a standard whereby the manufacturer is made the "guarantor" of the product's safety. Another appears to apply a consumer-expectation test that has no risk-utility component. These opinions are not consistent with the rule stated in this section.

i. Categorical design liability not recognized. By referring explicitly to risk reduction through the adoption of a reasonable-cost, safer design, subsection (2)(b) makes clear that the social risk-utility balancing employed in judging the reasonableness of product designs will not be undertaken on a categorical basis. For the purposes of this analysis, product categories are relatively broad subsets of products for which, given their inherent design characteristics, no adequate alternatives are available. Examples include alcoholic beverages, tobacco products, handguns, and above-ground swimming pools. With respect to a product in such a category, plaintiffs are unable to prove the availability of a safer design that does not eliminate the inherent characteristic that renders the product and other similar products attractive in the marketplace. For example, removing the alcohol from an alcoholic beverage not only removes the product from the category of alcoholic beverages, but also renders it unattrative to most consumers of alcoholic beverages. Alcohol-free "alcoholic beverages" are not, therefore, available to most consumers at "reasonable cost." A plaintiff could attack such a product for its alcoholic quality only by attacking the larger category of alcoholic beverages as somehow per se unreasonably dangerous, something that subsection (2)(b) disallows.

Although courts in a few jurisdictions have purportedly allowed plaintiffs to condemn broad product categories as unreasonably dangerous, those decisions have been overturned by statute. Virtually every American jurisdiction now rejects product category liability. The inherent risks associated with product categories are typically open and obvious, and can be adequately managed in the marketplace. Moreover, the legal and factual issues raised in categorical product design litigation are beyond the capacities of courts to resolve. Decisions regarding which product categories should generally be available to users and consumers are best left to the marketplace or, in rare instances, to government regulators other than courts.

Of course, when a plaintiff can establish that a manufacturing defect caused injury; that a product unit could have been designed more safely without eliminating the inherent characteristics that both define it categorically and make it desirable for use and consumption; or that a product unit could have been distributed with more adequate and useful instructions and warnings, then the rule stated in this section supports liability. But judicial attacks on product categories, as such, are not recognized.

j. Warning defects. Subsection (2)(c) embraces a rule of liability long recognized by American courts: product sellers have a duty to provide reasonable instructions or warnings about nonobvious risks of injury associated with their products whenever a reasonable person in the seller's position would have, or reasonably should have, known of such risks of injury and could have supplied instructions or warnings to someone in a position to act effectively on such information. In most cases, the duty is based on the seller's knowledge at the time of sale, but under special circumstances post-sale duties to warn, based on later-acquired knowledge, may arise.

In any event, risks that should be obvious to reasonable persons need not be instructed about or warned against. In determining whether a risk is sufficiently obvious not to require a warning, judges have an important initial role to play in screening cases and keeping clear cases from the jury. It is anticipated, however, that obviousness of risk will be accessed by the jury in all cases in which reasonable minds might differ.

Product warnings help to reduce risks when supplied to persons in positions to act effectively on that information. Thus, the persons to whom product warnings should be given typically include users and consumers, but also include anyone who a reasonable distributor should know is in a position to respond to the instruction or warning by reducing or eliminating the risk of injury. The requirement in subsection 402A(1) that the defective condition be shown to have "proximately caused" the harm to persons or property imposes on plaintiffs in warning cases the burden of proving that, if an adequate instruction or warning had been supplied, use and consumption would have been altered so as to reduce or eliminate the plaintiff's injury.

k. Prescription drugs. Subject to the limitation recognized in comment *i,* courts may legitimately entertain causes of action based on most claims of defective product design. Notwithstanding this general rule, the overwhelming majority of jurisdictions have taken the position that a court is not to substitute its judgment for that of the prescribing physician regarding the design of a prescription drug. As long as the drug is marketed with warnings that adequately inform the prescribing physician of the drug's foreseeable dangers, the manufacturer is not held to the risk-utility standard set forth in subsection (2)(b). The position stated in this Comment applies to all prescription drugs as a matter of law, requiring no case-by-case examination of the risks and benefits of individual prescription drugs that are the subject of litigation.

III.   Author's Notes

A.   General Observations

If the truth be known, section 402A as originally drafted was not really a restatement of existing law. Products liability was in its infancy when the American Law Institute (ALI) promulgated this most important provision. No one, for example, could have foreseen that language written primarily to govern manufacturing defect cases might be used by courts in design and warning defect cases. The common law rules governing design and warning defect litigation were still heavily mired in the limited-duty setting of the previous half-century. Nor could anyone have foreseen the difficult causation problems that would arise with regard to defendant identification. The list of unresolved issues could go on and on. In any event, as a prestatement, section 402A served as a marvelous catalyst to change. It shook American courts out of their doldrums and invited them to re-examine many premises that stood as impediments to plaintiff recovery. "Strict liability" became more than a legal doctrine. It was the clarion call for a liability system free of artificial and often wooden restraints on liability. Faced with substantial authority to the contrary, plaintiffs could point to section 402A and argue with relative impunity that the old rules governed only the universe of negligence. Strict liability was different.

A quarter century has passed. The pace of American products liability litigation has been fast and furious. We can say with some confidence that if we have not yet seen all the problems raised in such litigation, we have seen most of them. It is also fair to say that although courts continue to differ on many issues, enormous consensus has evolved regarding fundamental questions. This consensus requires further description and elaboration. First, on many issues there is simply broad-based, flat-out agreement as to doctrine. Second, in those instances in which courts differ with respect to doctrine, careful analysis reveals that despite the somewhat different verbalizations, the core approaches to the underlying problems are remarkably similar. Third, even where underlying differences can be substantitated, the practical implications for litigants often turn out to be smaller than they seem at first. Finally, we believe that some of the disagreement is the product of a fragmented approach to the subject matter. In the absence of a thorough and easily articulated alternate standard, courts often opt to go their own way, carving out a separate niche for themselves. In short, the time is ripe for a true restatement of products liability law.

We make no bones about it. We have drafted our proposed revision of section 402A to reflect a broad consensus view. When faced with a choice of drafting language in either the black letter text or the comments that introduces nuanced conflict or reflects consensus, we have opted for the latter. If courts in the future wish to debate the niceties and fine points, that is their prerogative. This proposed revision of section 402A, were it eventually to be adopted, would not stand in their way. But we hope the courts will also come to realize that beyond the minor points of disagreement stands a rather imposing doctrinal structure to which almost all pay allegiance.

In drafting our proposed revision, we face a logistical problem of considerable magnitude. Over the past decade thirty-eight state legislatures have passed statutes dealing with product liability law as part of their tort reform proposals. Had we sought to account for all the differences among states, it would have been impossible to draft a restatement. However, by dealing with broad consensus principles, it is possible to embrace a basic structure without running afoul of the state statutes. For the most part, products liability reform statutes do not stake out new principles of law; rather, they constitute adaptations of fundamental principles, each setting forth its own nuances. Thus, most reform statutes fit nicely into our revised black letter restatement of existing law.

Products liability mavens will note that we have not dealt with or commented upon every controversial issue in products liability law. We acknowledge that we have omitted many issues from our discussion. To do otherwise would require that we abandon our effort to write a restatement and instead author a treatise on the law of products liability. On the other hand, we have taken firm positions on a number of central issues, especially when the comments are taken into account. By definition, a restatement challenges the writer to outline the widely accepted principles that govern an area of the law. Others working from our proposal may challenge the wisdom of any given omission. Such debate is welcome, with the proviso that the sum of suggested additions not undo the effort to restate the law in a manner that is both useful to and useable by the bench and bar. It would be helpful to bear in mind that if efforts to revise section 402A fail, the alternative is the retention of an outdated and misleading section 402A—one that might have been a work of art in the era of violent change that followed its adoption, but which is today incapable of reflecting the reality of literally thousands upon thousands of decided cases.

B.   Liability for Failure to Instruct and Warn

Page 799.   Before Problem 40, add the following case:

Anderson v. Owens-Corning Fiberglas Corp.
53 Cal. 3d 987, 810 P.2d 549, 281 Cal. Rptr. 528 (1991)

PANELLI, J. Defendants are or were manufacturers of products containing asbestos. Plaintiff Carl Anderson filed suit in 1984, alleging that he contracted asbestosis and other lung ailments through exposure to asbestos and asbestos products (i.e., preformed blocks, cloth and cloth tape, cement, and floor tiles) while working as an electrician at the Long Beach Naval Shipyard from 1941 to 1976. Plaintiff allegedly encountered asbestos while working in the vicinity of others who were removing and installing insulation products aboard ships. . . .

Plaintiff's amended complaint alleged a cause of action in strict liability for the manufacture and distribution of "asbestos, and other products containing said substance . . . which caused injury to users and consumers, including plaintiff." . . . Plaintiff alleged that defendants marketed their products with specific prior knowledge, from scientific studies and medical data, that there was a high risk of injury and death from exposure to asbestos or asbestos-containing products; that defendants knew consumers and members of the general public had no knowledge of the potentially injurious nature of asbestos; and that defendants failed to warn users of the risk of danger. Defendants' pleadings raised the state-of-the-art defense, i.e., that even those at the vanguard of scientific knowledge at the time the products were sold could not have known that asbestos was dangerous to users in the concentrations associated with defendants' products.

Plaintiff moved before trial to prevent defendants from presenting state-of-the-art evidence. . . . The trial court granted the motion. . . . The defendants then moved to prevent plaintiff from proceeding on the failure-to-warn theory. . . . In response to the court's request for an offer of proof on the alleged failure to warn, plaintiff referred to catalogs and other literature depicting workers without respirators or protective devices and offered to prove that, until the mid-1960's, defendants had given no warnings of the dangers associated with asbestos, that various warnings given by some of the defendants after 1965 were inadequate, and, finally, that defendants removed the products from the market entirely in the early 1970's. Defendants argued in turn that the state of the art, i.e., what was scientifically knowable in the period 1943-1974, was their obvious and only defense to any cause of action for failure to warn, and that, in view of the court's decision to exclude state-of-the-art evidence, fairness dictated that plaintiff be precluded from proceeding on that theory. With no statement of reasons, the trial court granted defendants' motion. . . . After a four-week trial, the jury returned a verdict for defendants. . . .

Plaintiff moved for a new trial, asserting that the court erred in precluding proof of liability on a failure-to-warn theory. . . . The court granted the motion. . . . Plaintif . . . urged that knowledge or knowability, and thus state-of-the-art evidence, was irrelevant in strict liability for failure to warn. . . . The trial court agreed.

The Court of Appeal, in a two-to-one decision, upheld the order granting a new trial. . . . The appellate court added that, "in strict liability asbestos cases, including those prosecuted on a failure to warn theory, state of the art evidence is not admissible since it focuses on the reasonableness of the defendant's conduct, which is irrelevant in strict liability." The dissenting justice urged that the majority had imposed "absolute liability," contrary to the tenets of the strict liability doctrine, and that the manufacturers' right to a fair trial included the right to litigate all relevant issues, including the state of the art of scientific knowledge at the relevant time. We granted review. . . .

Failure to Warn Theory of Strict Liability . . .

In Cavers v. Cushman Motor Sales, Inc. (1979) 95 Cal. App. 3d 338, 157 Cal. Rptr. 142, the first case in which failure to warn was the sole theory of liability, the appellate court approved the instruction that a golf cart, otherwise properly manufactured, could be defective if no warning was given of the cart's propensity to tip over when turning and if the absence of the warning rendered the product substantially dangerous to the user. *Cavers* was principally concerned with the propriety of the term "substantially dangerous" and concluded that it is necessary to weigh the degree of danger involved when determining whether a warning defect exists.

[Early] cases did not address the specific factual question whether or not the manufacturer or distributor knew or should have known of the risks involved in the products, either because the nature of the product or the risk involved made such a discussion unnecessary or because the plaintiff limited the action to risks about which the manufacturer/distributor obviously knew or should have known. Moreover, the appellate courts in these same cases did not discuss knowledge or knowability as a component of the failure to warn theory of strict liability. However, a knowledge or knowability component clearly was included as an implicit condition of strict liability. In that regard, California was in accord with authorities in a majority of other states.

Only when the danger to be warned against was "unknowable" did the knowledge component of the failure-to-warn theory come into focus. Such cases made it apparent that eliminating the knowledge component had the effect of turning strict liability into absolute liability.

[The court reviews other California Court of Appeals decisions.]

In sum, the foregoing review of the decisions of the Courts of Appeal persuades us that California is well settled into the majority view that knowledge, actual or constructive, is a requisite for strict liability for failure to warn and that [our earlier decision], if not directly, at least by implication, reaffirms that position.

However, even if we are implying too much from the language in [our earlier decision,] the fact remains that we are now squarely faced with the issue of knowledge and knowability in strict liability for failure to warn in other than the drug context. Whatever the ambiguity of [our earlier decision,] we hereby adopt the requirement, as propounded by the Restatement Second of Torts and acknowledged by the lower courts of this state and the majority of jurisdictions, that knowledge or knowability is a component of strict liability for failure to warn.

One of the guiding principles of the strict liability doctrine was to relieve a plaintiff of the evidentiary burdens inherent in a negligence cause of action. . . . Indeed, it was the limitations of negligence theories that prompted the development and expansion of the doctrine. The proponents of the minority rule, including the Court of Appeal in this case, argue that the knowability requirement, and admission of state-of-the-art evidence, improperly infuse negligence concepts into strict liability cases by directing the trier of fact's attention to the conduct of the manufacturer or distributor rather than to the condition of the product. Similar claims have been made as to other aspects of strict liability, sometimes resulting in limitations on the doctrine and sometimes not.

[The court discusses earlier decisions not involving failure to warn.]

As these cases illustrate, the strict liability doctrine has incorporated some well-settled rules from the law of negligence and has survived judicial challenges asserting that such incorporation violates the fundamental principles of the doctrine. It may also be true that the "warning defect" theory is "rooted in negligence" to a greater extent than are the manufacturing- or design-defect theories. The "warning defect" relates to a failure extraneous to the product itself. Thus, while a manufacturing or design defect can be evaluated without reference to the conduct of the manufacturer . . . the giving of a warning cannot. The latter necessarily requires the communicating of something to someone. How can one warn of something that is unknowable? If every product that has no warning were defective per se and for that reason subject to strict liability, the mere fact of injury by an unlabelled product would automatically permit recovery. That is not, and has never been, the purpose and goal of the failure-to-warn theory of strict liability. Further, if a warning automatically precluded liability in every case, a manufacturer or distributor could easily escape liability with overly broad, and thus practically useless, warnings. . . .

We therefore reject the contention that every reference to a feature shared with theories of negligence can serve to defeat limitations on the doctrine of strict liability. Furthermore, despite its roots in negligence, failure to warn in strict liability differs markedly from failure to warn in the negligence context. Negligence law in a failure-to-warn case requires a plaintiff to prove that a manufacturer or distributor did not warn of a particular risk for reasons which fell below the acceptable standard of care, i.e., what a reasonably prudent manufacturer would have known and warned about. Strict liability is not concerned with the standard of due care or the reasonableness of a manufacturer's conduct. The rules of strict liability require a plaintiff to prove only that the defendant did not adequately warn of a particular risk that was known or knowable in light of the generally recognized and prevailing best scientific and medical knowledge available at the time of manufacture and distribution. Thus, in strict liability, as opposed to negligence, the reasonableness of the defendant's failure to warn is immaterial.

Stated another way, a reasonably prudent manufacturer might reasonably decide that the risk of harm was such as not to require a warning as, for example, if the manufacturer's own testing showed a result contrary to that of others in the scientific community. Such a manufacturer might escape liability under negligence principles. In contrast, under strict liability principles the manufacturer has no such leeway; the manufacturer is liable if it failed to give warning of dangers that were known to the scientific community at the time it manufactured or distributed the product. Whatever may be reasonable from the point of view of the manufacturer, the user of the product must be given the option either to refrain from using the product at all or to use it in such a way as to minimize the degree of danger. Davis v. Wyeth Laboratories, Inc. (9th Cir. 1968) 399 F.2d 121, 129-130, described the need to warn in order to provide "true choice": "When, in a particular case, the risk qualitatively (e.g., of death or major disability) as well as quantitatively, on balance with the end sought to be achieved, is such as to call for a true choice judgment, medical or personal, the warning must be given. [Footnote omitted.]"

. . . Thus, the fact that a manufacturer acted as a reasonably prudent manufacturer in deciding not to warn, while perhaps absolving the manufacturer of liability under the negligence theory, will not preclude liability under strict liability principles if the trier of fact concludes that, based on the information scientifically available to the manufacturer, the manufacturer's failure to warn rendered the product unsafe to its users.

The foregoing examination of the failure-to-warn theory of strict liability in California compels the conclusion that knowability is relevant to imposition of liability under that theory. Our conclusion not only accords with precedent but also with the considerations of policy that underlie the doctrine of strict liability.

We recognize that an important goal of strict liability is to spread the risks and costs of injury to those most able to bear them. However, it was never the intention of the drafters of the doctrine to make the manufacturer or distributor the insurer of the safety of their products. It was never their intention to impose absolute liability.

Conclusion

Therefore, in answer to the question raised in our order granting review, a defendant in a strict products liability action based upon an alleged failure to warn of a risk of harm may present evidence of the state of the art, i.e., evidence that the particular risk was neither known nor knowable by the application of scientific knowledge available at the time of manufacture and/or distribution. The judgment of the Court of Appeal is affirmed with directions that the matter be remanded to the trial court for proceedings in accord with our decision herein.

LUCAS, C.J., and KENNARD, ARABIAN and BAXTER, JJ., concur. . . .

MOSK, J., concurring and dissenting.

In my view the trial court properly granted a new trial and the Court of Appeal, in a thoughtful analysis of the law, correctly affirmed the order. I thus concur in the result.

I must express my apprehension, however, that we are once again retreating from "[t]he pure concepts of products liability so pridefully fashioned and nurtured by this court." (Daly v. General Motors Corp. (1978) 20 Cal. 3d 725, 757, 144 Cal. Rptr. 380, 575 P.2d 1162 (dis. opn. by Mosk, J.).) . . .

The majority distinguish failure-to-warn strict liability claims from negligence claims on the ground that strict liability is not concerned with a standard of due care or the reasonableness of a manufacturer's conduct. This is generally accurate. However in practice this is often a distinction without a substantial difference. Under either theory, imposition of liability is conditioned on the defendant's actual or constructive knowledge of the risk. Recovery will be allowed only if the defendant has such knowledge yet fails to warn. . . .

We should consider the possibility of holding that failure-to-warn actions lie solely on a negligence theory. "[A]lthough mixing negligence and strict liability concepts is often a game of semantics, the game has more than semantic impact—it breeds confusion and inevitably, bad law." (Henderson & Twerski, Doctrinal Collapse in Products Liability: The Empty Shell of Failure to Warn, 65 N.Y.U. L. Rev. at p. 278.) If, however, the majority are not ready to take that step, I would still use this opportunity to enunciate a bright-line rule to apply in failure-to-warn strict liability actions.

Here plaintiff alleged, among other claims, that defendants marketed their products "with specific prior knowledge" of the high risks of injury and death from their use. If plaintiff can establish at the new trial that defendants had actual knowledge, then state of the art evidence—or what everyone else was doing at the time—would be irrelevant and the trial court could properly exclude it. Actual knowledge may often be difficult to prove, but it is not impossible with adequately probing discovery. Defendants, of course, can produce evidence that they had no such prior actual knowledge.

On the other hand, if plaintiff is only able to show, by medical and scientific data or other means, that defendants should have known of the risks inherent in their products, then contrary medical and scientific data and state of the art evidence would be admissible if offered by defendants.

Thus I would draw a clear distinction in failure-to-warn cases between evidence that the defendants had actual knowledge of the dangers and evidence that the defendants should have known of the dangers.

With the foregoing rule in mind, the parties should proceed to the new trial ordered by the trial court and upheld by the Court of Appeal. Thus I would affirm the judgment of the Court of Appeal.

Chapter 11

Dignitary Wrongs, Intentional Infliction of Mental Upset, and Violations of Civil Rights

B. Offensive Battery

Page 968.   After Problem 43, add the following case:

Funeral Services by Gregory, Inc. v. Bluefield Community Hospital
413 S.E.2d 79 (W. Va. 1991)

BROTHERTON, Justice: In this case, we are asked to determine whether a mortician who embalmed a corpse, unaware that it was infected with Acquired Immune Deficiency Syndrome, was subjected to a battery. The appellants, Keith Gregory and his wife, Cassandra Miller Gregory, appeal from August 17, 1989, and November 14, 1989, rulings of the Circuit Court of Mercer County which dismissed all of their claims against the appellees, Bluefield Community Hospital, Dr. Naeem Qazi, and other unnamed individuals.

Keith Gregory is a mortician who embalmed the body of "John Doe," a man who died at Bluefield Community Hospital on June 5, 1986. According to the hospital, when John Doe was admitted on May 25, 1986, the only medical history he reported was having had pneumonia in the past week and using antibiotics. He denied ever having any major medical problems.

However, on the day of John Doe's funeral, June 11, 1986, Gregory learned from the hospital that John Doe was infected with the Acquired Immune Deficiency Syndrome (hereinafter referred to as AIDS) at the time of his death. Nearly two years later, on June 3, 1988, Gregory and his wife initiated a suit for damages in the amount of four million dollars against the appellees, seeking recovery for severe emotional distress under several theories, including battery, intentional and negligent infliction of emotional distress, and intentional and negligent misrepresentation.

The lower court dismissed all of Gregory's claims except the battery claim on August 17, 1989. The court concluded that all claims other than the battery claim were governed by the one-year statute of limitations found in W. Va. Code §55-2-12(c) and were therefore time-barred. On September 29, 1989, both parties moved for summary judgment on the remaining claim. By order dated November 14, 1989, the lower court granted the appellees' motion for summary judgment and dismissed the battery claim, indicating that the facts alleged by the Gregorys did not establish the type of harmful or offensive touching necessary to constitute a battery.

The facts contained in the record now before this Court reveal that after John Doe died on June 5, 1986, the hospital released the body to Kimball Funeral Home for embalming and funeral services. Michael Nowlin and Daniel Gregory, the plaintiff's brother, picked up the body at the hospital morgue. Hospital personnel told the men to wear protective gloves, masks, aprons, hats, and booties. Although they found these precautions a bit unusual, both men maintain that they were not told that John Doe was an AIDS-infected corpse, and that neither the toe tag on the body nor the death certificate mentioned AIDS as a possible cause of death. Nowlin and Daniel Gregory stated that the body was bloody because it had been subjected to a full autopsy, so they wrapped it in garbage bags to prevent it from soiling their cot and blanket any more than necessary. They subsequently delivered the body and the death certificate to the preparation room of the Gregory Funeral Home in Williamson, West Virginia.

The appellant, Keith Gregory, states that he was not unduly concerned when he began the embalming procedure on John Doe, because the death certificate did not list AIDS as a cause of death and the toe tag on the body did not indicate that an infectious disease was involved. However, after working on the body for about ninety minutes, Gregory took a break, at which time his brother Daniel related his perception that hospital personnel were acting strange in making him and Nowlin wear so much protective gear before removing the body. Gregory was suspicious, but because he did not want to stop in the middle of embalming the body, he went back to the preparation room and put on additional protective clothing.[2a] Upon completing the embalming procedure, he washed his arms with Clorox bleach and took his clothes off and later burned them. He immediately showered and then washed his hands and fingernails with Clorox.

2a. When he began the embalming procedure, Gregory states that he was wearing a surgical scrub suit, athletic socks, deck shoes, and latex surgical gloves. He later added a mask, rubber sleeves, shoe covers, and an additional apron.

As we noted above, on the morning of John Doe's funeral on June 11, 1986, the hospital called Keith Gregory and informed him that John Doe had probably died of AIDS. Gregory states that if he had known from the beginning that John Doe was infected with the AIDS virus, he would have suggested that the family arrange a burial within twenty-four hours, cremation, or a closed casket funeral service. These procedures would not require embalming the body. If the family had insisted upon embalming, Gregory would have taken steps to minimize his exposure, such as wearing additional protective clothing, asking another mortician to assist in the procedure in order to reduce preparation time, or sending the body to an embalming service.

Gregory and his wife allege that as a result of the appellees' tortious conduct, they now live with the fear that one or both of them will someday be diagnosed as having AIDS. The Gregorys state that they "have suffered severe emotional distress and humiliation, and their marriage has all but fallen apart."

Because Gregory did not file suit for damages until almost two years after he performed the embalming procedure on John Doe, he now asks this Court to find that the causes of action which he asserts against the defendants are subject to the two-year statute of limitations found in W. Va. Code §55-2-12(b). West Virginia Code §55-2-12(b) (1981) provides that "[c]very personal action for which no limitation is otherwise prescribed shall be brought . . . (b) within two years next after the right to bring the same shall have accrued if it be for damages for personal injuries; . . ."

Noting that this Court has held that damages for emotional distress may be recovered in a battery action, Criss v. Criss, 177 W. Va. 749, 356 S.E.2d 620 (1987), the appellant argues first that the lower court erred when it held that exposing someone to intimate physical contact with the bodily fluids and tissues of an AIDS-infected corpse, without his knowledge or consent, did not constitute an "offensive touching" sufficient to support a claim of battery. However, we agree that the appellees' actions cannot be construed as a battery, and find that the lower court properly granted summary judgment in favor of the appellees.

The Restatement (Second) of Torts, §13(a) and (b) (1965), states that: "[a]n actor is subject to liability to another for battery if (a) he acts intending to cause a harmful or offensive contact with the person of the other or a third person, or an imminent apprehension of such a contact, and (b) a harmful contact with the person of the other directly or indirectly results." The word "intent" in the Restatement denotes that "the actor desires to cause the consequences of his act, or that he believes that the consequences are substantially certain to result from it." Id. at §8A.

In this case, the hospital simply released the body to the plaintiff's funeral home for preparation. The plaintiff alleges that this act resulted in an "offensive touching" which constituted a battery, because he was subsequently "exposed to body fluids and mucus membranes of the deceased 'John Doe' which were infected with the AIDS virus thereby being exposed by the extreme and outrageous conduct of the defendants intentionally or recklessly to the AIDS virus. . . ." However, the plaintiff does not allege that the hospital acted with the intention of causing him a harmful or offensive contact, nor is there any evidence which might support such a charge. Whether the hospital negligently caused Gregory to come into contact with the body of John Doe is a separate inquiry.

We also note that the plaintiff did not allege that he suffered actual physical impairment as a result of what he refers to as an "exposure" to the AIDS virus.[2b] All of the plaintiffs' claims are based solely on a fear of contracting the AIDS virus. However, Gregory has been tested for AIDS antibodies on four occasions with negative results. Thus, there is no evidence that Gregory has been infected with the Human Immunodeficiency Virus (HIV), a retrovirus that causes AIDS. "It is extremely unlikely that a patient who tests HIV-negative more than six months after a potential exposure will contract the disease as a result of that exposure." Burk v. Sage Products, Inc., 747 F. Supp. 285, 287 (E.D. Pa. 1990), citing Morbidity and Mortality Weekly Report, July 21, 1989, Vol. 38, No. S-7 at 5.

Although the plaintiff undoubtedly came into contact with bodily fluids during the embalming procedure, there is no evidence indicating that he was actually exposed to a disease-causing agent. It is a well-established medical fact that the AIDS virus is transmitted through the exchange of bodily fluids, primarily blood or semen. The plaintiff admits that he was wearing proper protective gear, and he merely hypothesizes as to how a potential exposure to the virus may have occurred without offering any substantiating evidence.[2c] For example, the plaintiff did not recall sticking himself or puncturing his gloves during the embalming procedure.

Exposure to the AIDS virus was recently discussed by this Court in Johnson v. West Virginia University Hospitals, Inc., 413 S.E.2d 889 (W.

2b. Section 14 of the Restatement (Second) of Torts provides further that "[t]o make the actor liable for a battery, the harmful bodily contact must be caused by an act done by the person whose liability is in question." "Bodily harm" is defined as "any physical impairment of the condition of another's body, or physical pain or illness." Id. at §15.

2c. William Robinson, M.D., an expert retained by the Gregorys, stated in an affidavit that "to a reasonable degree of medical certainty" Gregory "was exposed to the AIDS virus as a result of the aerosolizing of the fluids of the corpse during the embalming process." When plaintiff's counsel raised this point with this Court during oral arguments, he was asked exactly how this may have resulted in an exposure, since Gregory had no open wounds or sores and was, in fact, wearing protective clothing. Counsel stated that Gregory had chapped lips, presumably implying that infected aerosols or droplets could have come into contact with chapped lips.

Va., November 21, 1991). In *Johnson,* we stated that "[t]here is no dispute that the AIDS-infected blood of the patient came into contact with the blood of the appellee. Expert testimony on behalf of the appellant acknowledged that this case involved an exposure." *Johnson,* 413 S.E.2d at 893. In upholding a jury award of $1.9 million to a police officer who was bitten by an AIDS-infected patient, we noted that, ". . . before a recovery for emotional distress damages may be made due to a fear of contracting a disease, such as AIDS, there must first be exposure to the disease. If there is no exposure, damages will be denied." Id., 413 S.E.2d at 893. Other courts have reached similar results.

For example, in Burk v. Sage Products, Inc., 747 F. Supp. 285 (E.D. Pa. 1990), the court noted that the plaintiff's claims "stem entirely from his fear of contracting AIDS as a result of the needle-stick injury." Id. at 286. However, the plaintiff could not prove that the needle which pricked him was a needle which was used on an AIDS patient. The court stated that:

> . . . plaintiff cannot show that he has been exposed to the AIDS virus. Plaintiff's position is in marked contrast to the other situations where recovery for fear of contracting a disease has been held compensable, in that plaintiff in this case is unable to demonstrate an exposure to a disease-causing agent. The cases which have allowed recovery for fear of disease have done so when the plaintiffs were faced only with the question of whether they would contract the disease in the future; the plaintiff in the instant case faces the additional question of whether he has been exposed to the AIDS virus in the first place. The court has been unable to locate a single case, from any jurisdiction, which has permitted recovery for emotional distress arising out of a fear of contracting disease when the plaintiff cannot prove exposure to the agent which has the potential to cause the disease.

Based upon our reading of these and other similar cases, as well as our own opinion in *Johnson,* we conclude that if a suit for damages is based solely upon the plaintiff's fear of contracting AIDS, but there is no evidence of an actual exposure to the virus, the fear is unreasonable, and this Court will not recognize a legally compensable injury.

For the reasons set forth above, the orders of the Circuit Court of Mercer County dismissing the appellants' claims are hereby affirmed.

Affirmed.

D.   Intentional Infliction of Mental Upset

Page 994.   After Meyer v. Nottger add the following new case:

Christensen v. The Superior Court
54 Cal. 3d 868, 820 P.2d 181, 2 Cal. Rptr. 2d 79 (Cal. 1991)

BAXTER, Justice. We are asked to decide whether persons other than those who contract for the services of mortuaries and crematoria or have the statutory right to direct the disposition of the body of a decedent may recover damages for emotional distress engendered by knowledge of the negligent or intentional mishandling of the decedent's remains when they did not observe the misconduct or its consequences. The Court of Appeal held that close family members may recover damages for the emotional distress they suffer if remains are negligently or intentionally mishandled, and that if the mishandling is intentional all family members and close friends of the deceased may [recover such damages].

We agree that the class of persons who may recover for emotional distress negligently caused by the defendants is not limited to those who have the statutory right to control disposition of the remains and those who contract for disposition. The class is not, however, as expansive as that identified by the Court of Appeal. As in all recovery for negligence, the potential plaintiff must be a person to whom the defendant owes a duty recognized by the law. In this context, the duty is owed only to close family members who were aware that funeral and/or crematory services were being performed, and on whose behalf or for whose benefit the services were rendered.

Therefore, and because we also conclude that the individual plaintiffs and the class they seek to represent lack standing to recover on an intentional infliction of emotional distress theory, the judgment of the Court of Appeal must be modified.

I

This matter arises on review of a ruling on standing to sue made by the trial court in a coordination proceeding. At the trial court's request the parties briefed the question of standing based on the allegations of a designated "model" complaint, selected for the purpose of preliminary rulings from those filed in the coordinated actions. The Court of Appeal treated the ruling as one in the nature of a ruling on a demurrer, accepting the allegations of the model complaint as true for purposes of this proceeding, and considering whether those allegations stated a cause of action on behalf of all of the individual plaintiffs, and the class the individual plaintiffs sought to represent.[4a]

In response to plaintiffs' petition for writ of mandate, after issuance of an alternative writ the Court of Appeal directed that a peremptory writ issue to compel the trial court to modify its order to recognize the standing of additional plaintiffs.

We agree with the Court of Appeal that the ruling, although described as one on standing, was in the nature of a ruling on a demurrer inasmuch as the effect was to determine whether all of the plaintiffs and the plaintiff class had stated a cause or causes of action for which each could recover emotional distress damages. We address the issues as having been raised in that context.

The model complaint defined the plaintiff class as one consisting of surviving spouses, relatives, and designated representatives of decedents whose remains had been mishandled by defendants. The individual plaintiffs who seek to represent the class are persons within the class who have the right and responsibility for handling, and the right to custody and possession of their decedents' remains, and possess or may acquire the right under section 7100 of the Health and Safety Code to control disposition of the remains, and/or contracted for defendants' services, paid for the services, or represent the estates of persons who did so.[4b]

All of the individual plaintiffs and members of the plaintiff class as described in the model complaint are, therefore, contracting parties and/or relatives of decedents whose remains were allegedly mishandled.

The defendants fall into two principal classes designated by plaintiffs as the "mortuary" defendants and the "crematory" defendants. The mortuary defendants allegedly undertook to, contracted to, and agreed to provide funeral-related services for the benefit of plaintiffs, and to accomplish the cremation of the remains of plaintiffs' decedents "with the dignity and respect due them in accordance with Plaintiffs' and decedents' wishes, in keeping with public sensibilities, and in accordance with the law." The mortuary defendants contracted with the crematory defendants for cremation of the remains.

The crematory defendants, who represented that they would perform cremations in a dignified and respectful manner, provided forms authorizing cremation to the mortuary defendants to enable the latter to obtain

---

4a. The action has not yet been certified as a class action. The trial court's request for briefing on the question of standing appears to have been made in anticipation of that ruling.

4b. The model complaint alleges that the plaintiff class consists of at least 6,050 members. Defendants state that the 15 coordinated lawsuits allege misconduct in the disposition of 16,500 decedents, thus creating a potential class of much greater magnitude.

consent from the next of kin whose business the mortuary defendants solicited on behalf of both themselves and the crematory defendants.

The mortuary defendants knew, or should have known, of the illegal and improper practices of the crematory defendants.

The remaining defendants, Carolina Biological Supply Company and its agent William G. Gabriel, residents of North Carolina (collectively, the Carolina defendants), allegedly requested and purchased human organs and body parts from the crematory defendants. The Carolina defendants failed to seek review of an earlier order of the trial court overruling their demurrer, and did not seek review of the Court of Appeal ruling on the standing of a subclass of plaintiffs who seek recovery from the Carolina defendants. In that ruling, the Court of Appeal held that only the statutory right holders may recover from the Carolina defendants that, allegedly, purchased bodily organs and parts taken from plaintiffs' decedents by the crematory defendants, and did so under circumstances in which the Carolina defendants knew or should have known that desecration of human remains would necessarily occur.

. . . The events about which plaintiffs complain occurred in the period 1980-1987, but were not discovered by plaintiffs until February 1987, when plaintiffs first learned "from public media reports" that their decedents' remains had been mishandled in the manner alleged in the complaint.

The model complaint alleged that the crematory defendants mishandled and mutilated remains, commingled human remains, and violated sections 7051, 7052, 7054.7, and 7055, as well as Business and Professions Code section 7735, and Penal Code section 487(1).

More specifically, in support of this allegation and one charging that those defendants had "removed and 'harvested,' without authorization or permission, numerous human organs and body parts from plaintiffs' decedents' remains," the complaint alleged that defendants cremated remains in the pottery kiln of defendant Oscar Ceramics; cremated remains in a disrespectful manner; cremated as many as 10 to 15 bodies together at the pottery kiln and multiple bodies at other locations; took and sold gold and other metals from the remains; placed cremated remains in urns or other containers without preserving their integrity or identity; and mutilated decedents' remains "including, but not limited to the unauthorized taking of Plaintiffs' decedents' corneas, eyes, hearts, lungs and other organs, and bones and body parts, which were sold for Defendants' profit. . . ."

The mortuary defendants, who had agreed to provide funeral-related services and accomplish cremation of the remains for the benefit of plaintiffs, had contracted with the crematory defendants for services in circumstances in which they knew or should have known that this conduct was occurring or would occur.

On discovering defendants' misconduct plaintiffs suffered and will continue to suffer "physical injury, shock, outrage, extreme anxiety, worry, mortification, embarrassment, humiliation, distress, grief, and sorrow."

The ninth cause of action, identified as one for "Intentional Interference with Remains and Infliction of Emotional Distress," alleged that the crematory and mortuary defendants had wilfully and deliberately interfered with the rights and duties of the plaintiffs to effect the proper cremation of the remains "by mutilating the remains by 'harvesting' of organs and body parts, by performing multiple cremations, by commingling decedents' cremated remains with other cremated remains, and with nonhuman residue, and by unceremoniously and disrespectfully handling Plaintiff's decedents' remains, rather than by separately, respectfully, and with dignity, handling the cremated remains. . . ." As a result plaintiffs allegedly suffered injury like that described above.

The 10th cause of action, identified as one for "Negligent Interference with Remains and Infliction of Emotional Distress," alleged the same improper conduct and injury caused by defendants' negligent, reckless and careless interference with the plaintiffs' statutory rights and responsibilities to dispose of the remains of their decedents. This count also alleged that defendants had cremated, handled, and treated their decedents' remains in ways unauthorized by plaintiffs and their decedents, which were contrary to their wishes, requests, and beliefs. Such negligent interference was accomplished through the common course and practice of unauthorized mutilation, improper cremation and commingling of remains. Negligent entrustment of the remains to persons unqualified to handle them was also alleged.

Citing Cohen v. Groman Mortuary, Inc. (1964) 231 Cal. App. 2d 1, 41 Cal. Rptr. 481, and Sinai Temple v. Kaplan (1976) 54 Cal. App. 3d 1103, 127 Cal. Rptr. 80, as controlling, the trial court ruled that only those plaintiffs who were entitled by section 7100 to control the disposition of their decedents' remains as of the date of the decedents' death, or who actually contracted for disposition, had standing to assert the claims set forth in the model complaint.

II

Section 7100 establishes rights and duties in the disposition of human remains, providing:

> The right to control the disposition of the remains of a deceased person, unless other directions have been given by the decedent, vests in, and the duty of interment and the liability for the reasonable cost of interment of such remains devolves upon the following in the order named:

(a) The surviving spouse.
(b) The surviving child or children of the decedent.
(c) The surviving parent or parents of the decedent.
(d) The person or persons respectively in the next degrees of kindred in the order named by the laws of California as entitled to succeed to the estate of the decedent.
(e) The public administrator when the deceased has sufficient assets.

Other statutory provisions relied on by plaintiffs and/or relevant to the claims made by plaintiffs include the following:

The person who has the section 7100 duty of interment is entitled to custody of the remains for that purpose, or if the remains are cremated for burial at sea. (§7102.)

Pursuant to the version of the Uniform Anatomical Gift Act (§7150 et seq.) in effect when this case arose, an individual had the primary right to make, permit, or refuse to permit the making of an anatomical gift. (Former §7151. See now §7150.5.) It was and is a felony to remove any part of any human remains from the place deposited while awaiting interment with the intent to sell it, unless written permission is given by the person who holds the section 7100 right. (§7051. See also Pen. Code, §367f.)

Section 7054.7 prohibits multiple cremation of remains and commingling of remains without the written permission of the section 7100 right holder, making violation of its provisions a misdemeanor. Section 7055 makes it a misdemeanor to remove remains from one primary registration district to another, except in a funeral director's conveyance, without a permit by the local registrar.

III

Before considering the causes of action for negligent and intentional interference with remains, the Court of Appeal addressed the plaintiffs' standing to seek recovery on a theory that plaintiffs, or some of them, were third party beneficiaries of a contract for mortuary services. It concluded that a section 7100 right holder is the only express beneficiary of a contract for mortuary services, and that if the contracting party was not the section 7100 right holder, only the holder of that right may be seen as an intended beneficiary of the contract. The section 7100 right did devolve according to the statutory scheme, however, if the holder at the date of the death of the decedent himself died.

After considering this court's recent decisions in Thing v. La Chusa

(1989) 48 Cal. 3d 644, 257 Cal. Rptr. 865, 771 P.2d 814, and Marlene F. v. Affiliated Psychiatric Medical Clinic, Inc. (1989) 48 Cal. 3d 583, 257 Cal. Rptr. 98, 770 P.2d 278, the Court of Appeal held that none of the plaintiffs could recover on either a negligent infliction of emotional distress or an intentional infliction of emotional distress theory. The court also held, however, that the allegations of the complaint stated a cause of action for negligent mishandling of a corpse, as recognized in Quesada v. Oak Hill Improvement Co. (1989) 213 Cal. App. 3d 596, 261 Cal. Rptr. 769, for which the close family members described in *Thing* and grandchildren may recover damages for emotional distress. A broader class, all family members and close friends, could recover for emotional distress suffered as a result of the intentional mishandling of remains.

In reaching these conclusions, the Court of Appeal applied well-settled principles governing the tort of negligence. The court recognized, as had this court in Marlene F. v. Affiliated Psychiatric Medical Clinic, Inc., supra, 48 Cal. 3d 583, 588, 257 Cal. Rptr. 98, 770 P.2d 278, that when damages are sought for negligently inflicted emotional distress, the tort is negligence regardless of the specific name that may be used to describe the tort, and that the elements of duty, breach of duty, causation and damages must be pleaded and proven.

The court reasoned that when a mortuary agrees to care for the remains of a decedent, a special relationship is created between the mortuary and the close family members of the decedent by virtue of the nature of the services the mortuary undertakes to perform. The mortuary's duty to properly discharge its responsibility of caring for the decedent runs to all persons with whom it has that special relationship, not just to the person who actually contracts for the services. It is foreseeable that a breach of that duty may cause severe emotional distress to members of the bereaved family.

In recognizing a broader class of persons entitled to recover for intentional mishandling of a corpse, the Court of Appeal relied on language in Amaya v. Home Ice, Fuel & Supply Co. (1963) 59 Cal. 2d 295, 315, 29 Cal. Rptr. 33, 379 P.2d 513, quoted with approval in Thing v. La Chusa, supra, 48 Cal. 3d 644, 652-653, 257 Cal. Rptr. 865, 771 P.2d 814, which distinguished the culpability and liability of intentional tortfeasors from that of those who are merely negligent:

> [T]he increased liability imposed on an intentional wrongdoer appears to reflect the psychological fact that solicitude for the interests of the actor weighs less in the balance as his [or her] moral guilt increases and the social utility of his [or her] conduct diminishes.

The Court of Appeal also reasoned, based on statements in Thing v. La Chusa, supra, 48 Cal. 3d 644, 257 Cal. Rptr. 865, 771 P.2d 814, that when an intentional tort is alleged, and society seeks to both punish the wrongdoer and deter such conduct by others, the imposition of liability out of all proportion to a defendant's negligence is not a concern. Therefore it is not necessary to limit liability to as narrow a class as is the case when negligence is the cause of the injury. For that reason, no arbitrary limitation of recovery to persons in a close family relationship with the decedent was required when the defendant had intentionally mishandled a corpse. Close friends of the decedent need not be denied the right to recover.

IV

[The Court's discussion of the negligence counts is omitted. After discussing the relevant precedents and public policies, the court concludes that close family members who were aware that funeral/crematory services were being performed, and who can show that their loved one's corpse was one of those actually mishandled, may recover. The court observes: "Defendants' purported liability to the relatives of more than 16,000 decedents is not a factor arising from a failure to narrow the class of potential plaintiffs. Rather it is a factor of the number of decedents whose remains defendants allegedly mishandled." (820 P.2d 200.)]

V   Intentional Infliction of Emotional Distress

There is merit in defendants' claim that the Court of Appeal erred in concluding that because the mishandling of the remains of plaintiffs' decedents was intentional and outrageous, all family members and close friends of the decedents could recover damages for emotional distress. The Court of Appeal reached that conclusion upon reasoning that defendants' conduct established the elements of the tort of intentional infliction of emotional distress.

The complaint does not allege, however, that any plaintiff was present when the misconduct occurred, or that defendants or any of them acted with the intent of causing emotional distress to the plaintiffs or knowledge that the conduct was substantially certain to cause distress to any particular plaintiff. The essence of the allegations is simply that the conduct was intentional, was outrageous, and was substantially certain to cause extreme emotional distress to relatives and close friends of the deceased.

The elements of the tort of intentional infliction of emotional distress are: " '(1) extreme and outrageous conduct by the defendant with the intention of causing, or reckless disregard of the probability of causing, emotional distress; (2) the plaintiff's suffering severe or extreme emotional distress; and (3) actual and proximate causation of the emotional distress by the defendant's outrageous conduct. . . .' Conduct to be outrageous must be so extreme as to exceed all bounds of that usually tolerated in a civilized community." (Davidson v. City of Westminster (1982) 32 Cal. 3d 197, 209, 185 Cal. Rptr. 252, 649 P.2d 894.) The defendant must have engaged in "conduct intended to inflict injury or engaged in with the realization that injury will result." (Id. at p. 210, 185 Cal. Rptr. 252, 649 P.2d 894.)

It is not enough that the conduct be intentional and outrageous. It must be conduct directed at the plaintiff, or occur in the presence of a plaintiff of whom the defendant is aware.

Past decisions of this court have invariably presupposed that the defendant's misconduct was directed to and was intended to cause severe or extreme emotional distress to a particular individual or, when reckless disregard was the theory of recovery, that the defendant directed his conduct at, and in conscious disregard of the threat to, a particular individual. In the seminal case permitting recovery even absent physical manifestation of the injury, State Rubbish etc. Assn. v. Siliznoff (1952) 38 Cal. 2d 330, 337, 240 P.2d 282, we observed that theretofore California had allowed recovery when "physical injury resulted from intentionally subjecting the plaintiff to serious mental distress." There, of course, agents of the defendant had intentionally caused the plaintiff to suffer extreme fright for the purpose of gaining a business advantage of the particular plaintiff.

Davidson v. City of Westminster, supra, 32 Cal. 3d 197, 185 Cal. Rptr. 252, 649 P.2d 894, is particularly instructive. There the plaintiff sought damages for intentional infliction of emotional distress based on the conduct of police officers who failed to intervene or protect her when they observed an assault suspect enter the public laundromat; the suspect had stabbed the plaintiff while the defendants had the premises under surveillance. We held that in the absence of an intent on the part of the defendant officers to injure the plaintiff, their conduct was not the kind of extreme and outrageous conduct that would give rise to liability for intentional infliction of emotional distress. (Id. at p. 210, 185 Cal. Rptr. 252, 649 P.2d 894.)

The requirement that the defendant's conduct be directed primarily at the plaintiff is a factor which distinguishes intentional infliction of emotional distress from the negligent infliction of such injury. We explained this distinction in Ochoa v. Superior Court [(1985)] 39 Cal. 3d 159, 216 Cal. Rptr. 661, 703 P.2d 1. There, the plaintiffs sought damages for the emotional distress they endured when over the course of several days they observed the deteriorating condition of their teenage son and the refusal of defendants to provide or permit them to provide needed medical treatment. Theories of negligent and intentional infliction of emotional distress were among the causes of action pled. This court held that while the complaint stated a cause of action for negligence, the elements of a cause of action for intentional infliction of emotional distress were not stated because the defendant's acts were directed at the child, not the parents.

> Plaintiffs appear to assume that a cause of action for intentional infliction of emotional distress may be established on the same theory as that for negligent infliction of emotional distress. The two torts are entirely different. . . .
>
>> A cause of action for intentional infliction of emotional distress must allege facts showing outrageous conduct which is intentional or reckless and which is outside the bounds of decency. It has been said in summarizing the cases discussing intentional infliction of emotional distress that "the rule which seems to have emerged is that there is liability for conduct exceeding all bounds usually tolerated by decent society, of a nature which is especially calculated to cause, and does cause, mental distress of a very serious kind." [Citations omitted.] Here, although defendants' conduct did cause the plaintiffs untold distress, it is evident that the defendants acted negligently rather than with the purpose of causing the plaintiffs emotional distress.

(39 Cal. 3d at p. 165, fn. 5, 216 Cal. Rptr. 661, 703 P.2d 1.)

In *Ochoa,* the defendants' conduct was directed primarily at plaintiffs' decedent. In concluding that recovery was not available under an intentional infliction of emotional distress theory, we noted that to the extent such recovery had been allowed, it has been limited to " 'the most extreme cases of violent attack, where there is some especial likelihood of fright or shock.' " (Id. at p. 165, fn. 5, 216 Cal. Rptr. 661, 703 P.2d 1. Accord, Coon v. Joseph (1987) 192 Cal. App. 3d 1269, 237 Cal. Rptr. 873.)

Recovery on an intentional infliction of emotional distress theory and based on reckless conduct has been allowed in the funeral-related services context. However, as Professors Prosser and Keeton note, the cases which describe the tort as intentional mishandling of a corpse actually seek to protect the personal feelings of the survivors. Therefore the tort is properly categorized as intentional infliction of emotional distress, and presupposes action directed at the plaintiff or undertaken with knowledge of the likelihood that the plaintiff will suffer emotional distress. (Prosser & Keeton, The Law of Torts, [(5th ed. 1984)] at pp. 60-63.) These authors acknowledge the problems associated with permitting recovery for action that is not directed at the plaintiff or undertaken with knowledge of the likelihood of harm to the plaintiff, noting the doctrine of transferred intent is inappropriate in this context. They suggest that to justify recovery the action must be directed to the plaintiff, and if reckless conduct is the basis for recovery, the plaintiff is usually present at the time of the conduct and is known by the defendant to be present.

We agree. "The law limits claims of intentional infliction of emotional distress to egregious conduct *toward plaintiff* proximately caused by defendant." (Miller v. National Broadcasting Co. (1986) 187 Cal. App. 3d 1463, 1489, 232 Cal. Rptr. 668. Italics added, original italics omitted.) The only exception to this rule is that recognized when the defendant is aware of, but acts with reckless disregard of the plaintiff and the probability that his conduct will cause severe emotional distress to that plaintiff. Where reckless disregard of the plaintiff's interests is the theory of recovery, the presence of the plaintiff at the time the outrageous conduct occurs is recognized as the element establishing a higher degree of culpability which, in turn, justifies recovery of greater damages by a broader group of plaintiffs than allowed on a negligent infliction of emotional distress theory.

Plaintiffs here have not alleged that the conduct of any of the defendants was directed primarily at them, was calculated to cause them severe emotional distress, or was done with knowledge of their presence and of a substantial certainty that they would suffer severe emotional injury. We conclude, therefore, that the model complaint does not establish that any of the plaintiffs has standing to sue for intentional infliction of emotional distress. Because this is a coordination proceeding, however, whether to permit further amendment should be left to the discretion of the trial court. . . .

VII Disposition

The judgment of the Court of Appeal is modified to direct the superior court to conform its order on standing to sue to reflect the views expressed herein.

LUCAS, C.J., and PANELLI, GEORGE and TURNER, JJ., concur.

MOSK, Justice, concurring and dissenting.

I agree with the majority that those close family members who were aware of both the decedent's death and the nature of the funeral services to be performed may state a claim for negligent infliction of emotional distress.[4c] I also agree that the power to control the disposition of remains

---

4c. Of course, exceptions to this general rule may arise. A close family member who is out of the country at the time of the decedent's death or who is in the hospital and not strong enough to hear the news may, in my view, be included in the plaintiff class.

devolves according to the priorities established by section 7100 of the Health and Safety Code.

I do not agree, however, that no plaintiffs may sue for intentional infliction of emotional distress (IIED) because the admittedly outrageous conduct was not directed primarily at them, nor did they witness it. It is paradoxical that the majority find defendants liable for negligent but not intentional conduct. The latter, being more reprehensible, should render the perpetrators liable to a greater rather than a lesser extent.

The majority assert that to require defendants to perform the acts in plaintiffs' presence ensures the high degree of culpability necessary to justify the greater damages allowed in an IIED case. In my view, if the acts alleged are found to be true, defendants are highly culpable regardless of whether plaintiffs witnessed the mutilation. I would allow the trier of fact to consider the issue of IIED.

Further, I would not limit the class of plaintiffs in IIED cases to blood relations. The issue of whether a person suffered severe distress is properly left to the trier of fact. We should not rule that, as a matter of law, a decedent's estranged sibling may have suffered emotional distress but not a decedent's close and longtime business partner.

I would allow plaintiffs to proceed on the IIED theory because defendants' alleged conduct was reckless. IIED may be shown in three ways: a subjective intention to cause emotional distress, a substantial certainty that such distress would result, or reckless behavior leading to emotional distress. The majority deny plaintiffs a cause of action for IIED because they did not allege that defendants' conduct "was directed primarily at them, was calculated to cause them severe emotional distress, or was done with knowledge of their presence and of a substantial certainty that they would suffer severe emotional injury."

Although defendants may have been motivated by profit rather than by a subjective desire to distress these plaintiffs, the trier of fact could still hold defendants liable on a reckless conduct theory. Recklessness may be found from acts "of an unreasonable character in disregard of a known or obvious risk that was so great as to make it highly probable that harm would follow." (Prosser & Keeton, The Law of Torts (5th ed. 1984) §34, p. 213.) IIED may be distinguished from negligent infliction of emotional distress (NIED) because recklessness requires a higher degree of fault than simple negligence.

The majority acknowledge that IIED may be shown from conduct undertaken with knowledge of the likelihood that the plaintiff will suffer emotional distress. If defendants in this emotionally charged occupation intentionally mutilated bodies and commingled remains, they necessarily realized that their conduct would cause the decedents' loved ones severe emotional distress.

The limits that the majority seek to place on the tort of IIED are, in this context, unjustified. To require that plaintiffs be present at the scene of the outrageous conduct is unrealistic. It will be a rare case indeed in which a funeral home mutilates a decedent's body in the presence of the grieving family or displays the mutilated body to them. The majority thus effectively limit a plaintiff's recourse in cases involving this type of reprehensible conduct to the lesser tort of NIED. Further, the majority's requirement that defendants consciously direct outrageous conduct at plaintiffs makes the "recklessness" prong indistinguishable from the "subjective intent" prong.

Other states' courts have found a cause of action for IIED under similar circumstances. For example, in Whitehair v. Highland Memory Gardens, Inc. (1985) 174 W. Va. 458, 327 S.E.2d 438, 440, the court held that the plaintiff could state a cause of action when the defendant mishandled the bodies of her sister, two aunts and a cousin during relocation of its cemetery. In Scarpaci v. Milwaukee County (1980) 96 Wis. 2d 663, 292 N.W.2d 816, 820, the court held that parents who alleged that the county wrongfully performed an autopsy on their son could state a claim for intentional interference with the right to bury their child. And in Carney v. Knollwood Cemetery Assn. (1986) 33 Ohio App. 3d 31, 514 N.E.2d 430, 435, the court held that the plaintiffs, who learned by a television broadcast that the grave of their ancestor had been disturbed, could state a claim for IIED. . . .

As the majority note, public policy considerations limit the right of a bystander to recover damages for the emotional distress suffered as a result of witnessing negligent conduct that causes physical injury to a third person: "If any and all bystanders who witnessed the injury-causing event were permitted to recover for ensuing emotional distress, the defendant's liability could be out of all proportion to the degree of fault."

The scope of liability for intentional infliction of emotional distress is not, however, limited by the same public policy dictates. As the Court of Appeal stated in this case, "an intentional wrongdoer is liable for a broad range of the effects of intentional acts. . . . Avoidance of liability out of all proportion to a defendant's negligence is not a concern when an intentional tort is alleged. As a society, we seek to punish the intentional wrongdoer and deter such conduct by others."

Further, I can find no public policy reason to limit the class of potential plaintiffs who may sue for IIED to family members. A longtime business associate should be allowed to present a case for IIED after a preliminary showing that he or she had a close relationship with the decedent. Proximate causation principles such as foreseeability do not belong in the analysis of an intentional tort. Of course, each plaintiff will have to prove all the elements of his or her case. I would merely hold that they should be permitted to so attempt.

Chapter 12

Defamation

B. The Constitutional Issues

Page 1069. *In the last paragraph, insert the following after the discussion of* **Goldwater v. Ginzberg:**

In Harte-Hanks Communications, Inc. v. Connaughton, 491 U.S. 657, 692, 109 S. Ct. 2678, 2698, 105 L. Ed. 2d 562, 591 (1989), the Court upheld a judgment for the plaintiff on the jury verdict for him, ruling that while failure of a reporter to investigate is not in itself enough to establish malice, the "purposeful avoidance of the truth is in a different category."

Page 1091. *Before* **Jacron Sales Co. v. Sindorf,** *add the following new case and text:*

Milkovich v. Lorain Journal Co.
110 S. Ct. 2695, 111 L. Ed. 2d 1 (1990)

Chief Justice REHNQUIST delivered the opinion of the Court. Respondent J. Theodore Diadiun authored an article in an Ohio newspaper implying that petitioner Michael Milkovich, a local high school wrestling coach, lied under oath in a judicial proceeding about an incident involving petitioner and his team which occurred at a wrestling match. Petitioner sued Diadiun and the newspaper for libel, and the Ohio Court of Appeals affirmed a lower court entry of summary judgment against petitioner. This judgment was based in part on the grounds that the article constituted an "opinion" protected from the reach of state defamation law by the First Amendment to the United States Constitution. We hold that the First Amendment does not prohibit the application of Ohio's libel laws to the alleged defamations contained in the article.

[The article that was the basis of the suit appeared in a newspaper owned by respondent Lorain Journal, and] bore the heading "Maple beat the law with the 'big lie,' " beneath which appeared Diadiun's photograph and the words "TD Says." The carryover page headline announced ". . . Diadiun says Maple told a lie." The column contained the following passages:

> . . . A lesson was learned (or relearned) yesterday by the student body of Maple Heights High School, and by anyone who attended the Maple-Mentor wrestling meet of last Feb. 8.
>
> A lesson which, sadly, in view of the events of the past year, is well they learned early.
>
> It is simply this: If you get in a jam, lie your way out.
>
> If you're successful enough, and powerful enough, and can sound sincere enough, you stand an excellent chance of making the lie stand up, regardless of what really happened.
>
> The teachers responsible were mainly Maple wrestling coach, Mike Milkovich, and former superintendent of schools, H. Donald Scott.
>
> Anyone who attended the meet, whether he be from Maple Heights, Mentor, or impartial observer, knows in his heart that Milkovich and Scott lied at the hearing after each having given his solemn oath to tell the truth.
>
> But they got away with it.
>
> Is that the kind of lesson we want our young people learning from their high school administrators and coaches?
>
> I think not.

Petitioner commenced a defamation action against respondents . . . alleging that the headline of Diadiun's article and the 9 passages quoted above "accused plaintiff of committing the crime of perjury, an indictable offense in the State of Ohio, and damaged plaintiff directly in his lifetime occupation of coach and teacher, and constituted libel per se."

[The Court's detailing of the proceedings below is omitted. The result of those proceedings is that summary judgment in favor of the respondents was affirmed on the ground that "the article in question was constitutionally protected opinion." Certiorari was granted "to consider the important questions raised by the Ohio courts' recognition of a constitutionally-required 'opinion' exception to the application of its defamation laws."] We now reverse.

Since the latter half of the 16th century, the common law has afforded a cause of action for damage to a person's reputation by the publication of false and defamatory statements.

In Shakespeare's Othello, Iago says to Othello:

> Good name in man and woman, dear my lord.
> Is the immediate jewel of their souls.

Who steals my purse steals trash;
'Tis something, nothing; 'Twas mine, 'tis his, and has been slave to
   thousands;
But he that filches from me my good name
Robs me of that which not enriches him,
And makes me poor indeed.

Act III, scene 3.

Defamation law developed not only as a means of allowing an individual to vindicate his good name, but also for the purpose of obtaining redress for harm caused by such statements. As the common law developed in this country, apart from the issue of damages, one usually needed only allege an unprivileged publication of false and defamatory matter to state a cause of action for defamation. The common law generally did not place any additional restrictions on the type of statement that could be actionable. Indeed, defamatory communications were deemed actionable regardless of whether they were deemed to be statements of fact or opinion. See, e.g., Restatement of Torts, §§565-567. As noted in the 1977 Restatement (Second) of Torts §566, Comment *a*:

> Under the law of defamation, an expression of opinion could be defamatory if the expression was sufficiently derogatory of another as to cause harm to his reputation, so as to lower him in the estimation of the community or to deter third persons from associating or dealing with him. . . . The expression of opinion was also actionable in a suit for defamation, despite the normal requirement that the communication be false as well as defamatory. . . . This position was maintained even though the truth or falsity of an opinion—as distinguished from a statement of fact—is not a matter that can be objectively determined and truth is a complete defense to a suit for defamation.

However, due to concerns that unduly burdensome defamation laws could stifle valuable public debate, the privilege of "fair comment" was incorporated into the common law as an affirmative defense to an action for defamation. "The principle of 'fair comment' afford[ed] legal immunity for the honest expression of opinion on matters of legitimate public interest when based upon a true or privileged statement of fact." 1 F. Harper & F. James, Law of Torts §5.28, p. 456 (1956) (footnote omitted). As this statement implies, comment was generally privileged when it concerned a matter of public concern, was upon true or privileged facts, represented the actual opinion of the speaker, and was not made solely for the purpose of causing harm. See Restatement of Torts, supra, §606. "According to the majority rule, the privilege of fair comment applied only to an expression of opinion and not to a false statement of fact,

whether it was expressly stated or implied from an expression of opinion."
Restatement (Second) of Torts, supra, §566, Comment *a*. Thus under the
common law, the privilege of "fair comment" was the device employed
to strike the appropriate balance between the need for vigorous public
discourse and the need to redress injury to citizens wrought by invidious
or irresponsible speech.

[The Court's discussion of the earlier Supreme Court cases imposing
constitutional restraints on the common law of defamation is omitted.]

Respondents would have us recognize, in addition to the established
safeguards discussed above, still another First Amendment-based protection for defamatory statements which are categorized as "opinion" as
opposed to "fact." For this proposition they rely principally on the
following dictum from our opinion in *Gertz* [v. Robert Welch, Inc., 418
U.S. 323, 94 S. Ct. 2997, 41 L. Ed. 2d 789 (1974)]:

> Under the First Amendment there is no such thing as a false idea. However
> pernicious an opinion may seem, we depend for its correction not on the
> conscience of judges and juries but on the competition of other ideas. But •
> there is no constitutional value in false statements of fact.

418 U.S., at 339-340, 94 S. Ct., at 3007 (footnote omitted).

Read in context, . . . the fair meaning of the passage is to equate the
word "opinion" in the second sentence with the word "idea" in the first
sentence. Under this view, the language was merely a reiteration of Justice
Holmes' classic "marketplace of ideas" concept. See Abrams v. United
States, 250 U.S. 616, 630, 40 S. Ct. 17, 22, 63 L. Ed. 1173 (1919) (Holmes,
J., dissenting) ("[T]he ultimate good desired is better reached by free
trade in ideas . . . the best test of truth is the power of the thought to
get itself accepted in the competition of the market").

Thus we do not think this passage from *Gertz* was intended to create
a wholesale defamation exemption for anything that might be labeled
"opinion.". . . Not only would such an interpretation be contrary to the
tenor and context of the passage, but it would also ignore the fact that
expressions of "opinion" may often imply an assertion of objective fact.

If a speaker says, "In my opinion John Jones is a liar," he implies a
knowledge of facts which lead to the conclusion that Jones told an untruth.
Even if the speaker states the facts upon which he bases his opinion, if
those facts are either incorrect or incomplete, or if his assessment of them
is erroneous, the statement may still imply a false assertion of fact. Simply
couching such statements in terms of opinion does not dispel these implications; and the statement, "In my opinion Jones is a liar," can cause
as much damage to reputation as the statement, "Jones is a liar." . . .

Apart from their reliance on the *Gertz* dictum, respondents do not really contend that a statement such as, "In my opinion John Jones is a liar," should be protected by a separate privilege for "opinion" under the First Amendment. But they do contend that in every defamation case the First Amendment mandates an inquiry into whether a statement is "opinion" or "fact," and that only the latter statements may be actionable. They propose that a number of factors developed by the lower courts (in what we hold was a mistaken reliance on the *Gertz* dictum) be considered in deciding which is which. But we think the " 'breathing space' " which " 'freedoms of expression require in order to survive,' " is adequately secured by existing constitutional doctrine without the creation of an artificial dichotomy between "opinion" and fact.

Foremost . . . a statement on matters of public concern must be provable as false before there can be liability under state defamation law, at least in situations, like the present, where a media defendant is involved. Thus, unlike the statement, "In my opinion Mayor Jones is a liar," the statement, "In my opinion Mayor Jones shows his abysmal ignorance by accepting the teachings of Marx and Lenin," would not be actionable. . . . [A] statement of opinion relating to matters of public concern which does not contain a provably false factual connotation will receive full constitutional protection.

Next, [protection is provided] for statements that cannot "reasonably [be] interpreted as stating actual facts" about an individual. . . . This provides assurance that public debate will not suffer for lack of "imaginative expression" or the "rhetorical hyperbole" which has traditionally added much to the discourse of our Nation.

The *New York Times-Butts* and *Gertz* culpability requirements further ensure that debate on public issues remains "uninhibited, robust, and wide-open," New York Times [Co. v. Sullivan], 376 U.S., at 270, 84 S. Ct., at 720 [(1964)]. Thus, where a statement of "opinion" on a matter of public concern reasonably implies false and defamatory facts regarding public figures or officials, those individuals must show that such statements were made with knowledge of their false implications or with reckless disregard of their truth. Similarly, where such a statement involves a private figure on a matter of public concern, a plaintiff must show that the false connotations were made with some level of fault as required by *Gertz*.

We are not persuaded that, in addition to these protections, an additional separate constitutional privilege for "opinion" is required to ensure the freedom of expression guaranteed by the First Amendment. The dispositive question in the present case then becomes whether or not a reasonable factfinder could conclude that the statements in the Diadiun column imply an assertion that petitioner Milkovich perjured himself in a judicial proceeding. We think this question must be answered in the affirmative. . . . This is not the sort of loose, figurative or hyperbolic language which would negate the impression that the writer was seriously maintaining petitioner committed the crime of perjury. Nor does the general tenor of the article negate this impression.

We also think the connotation that petitioner committed perjury is sufficiently factual to be susceptible of being proved true or false. A determination of whether petitioner lied in this instance can be made on a core of objective evidence by comparing, *inter alia,* petitioner's testimony [in two proceedings below.]

The numerous decisions discussed above establishing First Amendment protection for defendants in defamation actions surely demonstrate the Court's recognition of the Amendment's vital guarantee of free and uninhibited discussion of public issues. But there is also another side to the equation; we have regularly acknowledged the "important social values which underlie the law of defamation," and recognize that "[s]ociety has a pervasive and strong interest in preventing and redressing attacks upon reputation." Rosenblatt v. Baer, 383 U.S. 75, 86, 86 S. Ct. 669, 676, 15 L. Ed. 2d 597 (1966). Justice Stewart in that case put it with his customary clarity:

> The right of a man to the protection of his own reputation from unjustified invasion and wrongful hurt reflects no more than our basic concept of the essential dignity and worth of every human being—a concept at the root of any decent system of ordered liberty.
>
> The destruction that defamatory falsehood can bring is, to be sure, often beyond the capacity of the law to redeem. Yet, imperfect though it is, an action for damages is the only hope for vindication or redress the law gives to a man whose reputation has been falsely dishonored.

Id., at 92-93, 86 S. Ct., at 679-680 (Stewart, J., concurring).

We believe our decision in the present case holds the balance true. The judgment [below] is reversed and the case remanded for further proceedings not inconsistent with this opinion.

Reversed.

Justice BRENNAN, with whom Justice MARSHALL joins, dissenting.

Since this Court first hinted that the First Amendment provides some manner of protection for statements of opinion, notwithstanding any common-law protection, courts and commentators have struggled with the contours of this protection and its relationship to other doctrines within our First Amendment jurisprudence. Today, for the first time, the Court addresses this question directly and, to my mind, does so cogently and almost entirely correctly. I agree with the Court that . . . only defamatory statements that are capable of being proved false are subject to liability under state libel law. . . . I also agree with the Court that the "statement" that the plaintiff must prove false . . . is not invariably the literal phrase published but rather what a reasonable reader would have understood the author to have said.

In other words, while the Court today dispels any misimpression that there is a so-called opinion privilege wholly in addition to the protections we have already found to be guaranteed by the First Amendment, it determines that a protection for statements of pure opinion is dictated by existing First Amendment doctrine. As the Court explains, "full con-stitutional protection" extends to any statement relating to matters of public concern "that cannot 'reasonably [be] interpreted as stating actual facts' about an individual." Ante, at 2706. Among the circumstances to be scrutinized by a court in ascertaining whether a statement purports to state or imply "actual facts about an individual," as shown by the Court's analysis of the statements at issue here . . . are the same indicia that lower courts have been relying on for the past decade or so to distinguish between statements of fact and statements of opinion: the type of language used, the meaning of the statement in context, whether the statement is verifiable, and the broader social circumstances in which the statement was made.

With all of the above, I am essentially in agreement. I part company with the Court at the point where it applies these general rules to the statements at issue in this case because I find that the challenged state-ments cannot reasonably be interpreted as either stating or implying defamatory facts about petitioner. Under the rule articulated in the ma-jority opinion, therefore, the statements are due "full constitutional pro-tection." I respectfully dissent.

I

As the majority recognizes, the kind of language used and the context in which it is used may signal readers that an author is not purporting to state or imply actual, known facts.

Statements of belief or opinion are like hyperbole, as the majority agrees, in that they are not understood as actual assertions of fact about an individual, but they may be actionable if they imply the existence of false and defamatory facts. See ante, at 2706. The majority provides some general guidance for identifying when statements of opinion imply asser-tions of fact. . . . Although statements of opinion may imply an assertion of a false and defamatory fact, they do not invariably do so. Distinguishing which statements do imply an assertion of a false and defamatory fact requires the same solicitous and thorough evaluation that this Court has engaged in when determining whether particular exaggerated or satirical statements could reasonably be understood to have asserted such facts. As Justice Holmes observed long ago: "A word is not a crystal, transparent and unchanged, it is the skin of a living thought and may vary greatly in color and content according to the circumstances and time in which it is used." Towne v. Eisner, 245 U.S. 418, 425, 38 S. Ct. 158, 159, 62 L. Ed. 372 (1918).

For instance, the statement that "Jones is a liar," or the example given by the majority, "In my opinion John Jones is a liar"—standing alone— can reasonably be interpreted as implying that there are facts known to the speaker to cause him to form such an opinion. See ante, at 2705. But a different result must obtain if the speaker's comments had instead been as follows: "Jones' brother once lied to me; Jones just told me he was 25; I've never met Jones before and I don't actually know how old he is or anything else about him, but he looks 16; I think Jones lied about his age just now." In the latter case, there are at least six statements, two of which may arguably be actionable. The first such statement is factual and defamatory and may support a defamation action by Jones' brother. The second statement, however, that "I think Jones lied about his age just now," can be reasonably interpreted in context only as a statement that the speaker infers, from the facts stated, that Jones told a particular lie. It is clear to the listener that the speaker does not actually know whether Jones lied and does not have any other reasons for thinking he did. Thus, the only fact implied by the second statement is that the speaker drew this inference. If the inference is sincere or nondefamatory, the speaker is not liable for damages.

II

The majority does not rest its decision today on any finding that the statements at issue explicitly state a false and defamatory fact. Nor could it. Diadiun's assumption that Milkovich must have lied at the court hearing is patently conjecture. The majority finds Diadiun's statements actionable, however, because it concludes that these statements imply a factual assertion that Milkovich perjured himself at the judicial proceeding. I disagree. Diadiun not only reveals the facts upon which he is relying but he makes it clear at which point he runs out of facts and is simply guessing. Read in context, the statements cannot reasonably be interpreted as implying such an assertion as fact. . . .

No reasonable reader could understand Diadiun to be impliedly asserting—as fact—that Milkovich had perjured himself. Nor could such a reader infer that Diadiun had further information about Milkovich's court testimony on which his belief was based. It is plain from the column that Diadiun did not attend the court hearing. Diadiun also clearly had no detailed second-hand information about what Milkovich had said in court. Instead, what suffices for "detail" and "color" are quotations from the OHSAA hearing—old news compared to the court decision which prompted the column—and a vague quotation from an OHSAA commissioner. Readers could see that Diadiun was focused on the court's reversal of the OHSAA's decision and was angrily supposing what must have led to it.

Even the insinuation that Milkovich had repeated, in court, a more plausible version of the misrepresentations he had made at the OHSAA hearing is preceded by the cautionary term "apparently"—an unmistakable sign that Diadiun did not know what Milkovich had actually said in court. . . .

Furthermore, the tone and format of the piece notify readers to expect speculation and personal judgment. The tone is pointed, exaggerated and heavily laden with emotional rhetoric and moral outrage. Diadiun never says, for instance, that Milkovich committed perjury. He says that "[a]nyone who attended the meet . . . knows in his heart" that Milkovich lied—obvious hyperbole as Diadiun does not purport to have researched what everyone who attended the meet knows in his heart.

The format of the piece is a signed editorial column with a photograph of the columnist and the logo "TD Says." Even the headline on the page where the column is continued—"Diadiun says Maple told a lie," ante, at 2698— reminds readers that they are reading one man's commentary. While signed columns may certainly include statements of fact, they are also the "well recognized home of opinion and comment." Mr. Chow of New York v. Ste. Jour Azur S.A., 759 F.2d 219, 227 (CA2 1985). Certain formats—editorials, reviews, political cartoons, letters to the editor— signal the reader to anticipate a departure from what is actually known by the author as fact. . . .

III

Although I agree with the majority that statements must be scrutinized for implicit factual assertions, the majority's scrutiny in this case does not "hol[d] the balance true," ante, at 2708, between protection of individual reputation and freedom of speech. The statements complained of neither state nor imply a false assertion of fact and, under the rule the Court reconfirms today, they should be found not libel "as a matter of constitutional law." Ante, at 2704. Readers of Diadiun's column are signaled repeatedly that the author does not actually know what Milkovich said at the court hearing and that the author is surmising, from factual premises made explicit in the column, that Milkovich must have lied in court.

Like the "imaginative expression" and the "rhetorical hyperbole" which the Court finds "has traditionally added much to the discourse of our Nation," ante, at 2706, conjecture is intrinsic to "the free flow of ideas and opinions on matters of public interest and concern" that is at "the heart of the First Amendment." [Hustler Magazine v. Falwell, 485 U.S. 46, 50, 108 S. Ct. 876, 879 (1988)] The public and press regularly examine the activities of those who affect our lives. . . . But often only some of the facts are known, and solely through insistent prodding—through conjecture as well as research—can important public questions be subjected to the "uninhibited, robust, and wide-open" debate to which this country is profoundly committed. New York Times Co. v. Sullivan, 376 U.S. 254, 270, 84 S. Ct. 710, 720, 11 L. Ed. 2d 686 (1964).

Did NASA officials ignore sound warnings that the Challenger Space Shuttle would explode? Did Cuban-American leaders arrange for John Fitzgerald Kennedy's assassination? Was Kurt Waldheim a Nazi officer? Such questions are matters of public concern long before all the facts are unearthed, if they ever are. Conjecture is a means of fueling a national discourse on such questions and stimulating public pressure for answers from those who know more.

Diadiun, therefore, *is* guilty. He is guilty of jumping to conclusions, of benightedly assuming that court decisions are always based on the merits, and of looking foolish to lawyers. He is not, however, liable for defamation. Ignorance, without more, has never served to defeat freedom of speech. . . .

I appreciate this Court's concern with redressing injuries to an individual's reputation. But as long as it is clear to the reader that he is being offered conjecture and not solid information, the danger to reputation is one we have chosen to tolerate in pursuit of " 'individual liberty [and] the common quest for truth and the vitality of society as a whole.' " *Falwell,* supra, 485 U.S., at 50-51, 108 S. Ct., at 879. . . . Readers are as capable of independently evaluating the merits of such speculative conclusions as they are of evaluating the merits of pure opprobrium. Punishing such conjecture protects reputation only at the cost of expunging a genuinely useful mechanism for public debate. . . .

Milkovich has been seen as changing the law that made "opinion" immune to defamation litigation; that is, if the statement were defined as opinion, there could be no recovery in defamation based on it. See Anderson, Is Libel Law Worth Reforming?, 140 U. Pa. L. Rev. 487, 507

((1991). An example of the impact *Milkovich* has had on the courts is Unelko Corp. v. Rooney, 912 F.2d 1049 (9th Cir. 1990). In a nationally televised program, the defendant stated that he had tried a product made by the plaintiff called "Rain-X," advertized to be a "one-step, wipe-on automotive glass coating that repels rain, sleet and snow on contact and takes up where windshield wipers leave off!" The defendant stated over the air that he had tried the product and that "[i]t didn't work." In a decision rendered before *Milkovich,* the trial judge entered summary judgment in favor of the defendant on the ground that the statement was one of opinion, not of fact. The court of appeals disagreed with this assessment of the case, stating that "a factfinder could conclude that Rooney's statement that Rain-X 'didn't work' implied an assertion of objective fact." 912 F.2d at 1055. Perhaps the plaintiff should have left well enough alone, however, for the court of appeals affirmed the trial court, ruling that the plaintiff had failed to prove that the statement was false.

Milkovich does not, of course, preclude a state from according more protection to speech under state law than does the U.S. Supreme Court under the Constitution. In Immuno AG. v. J. Moor-Jankowski, 77 N.Y.2d 235, 567 N.E.2d 1270 (1991), the Court of Appeals of New York did extend broader protection to speech than did the court in *Milkovich.* The plaintiff sued the defendant, the editor of a scientific journal, for publishing a letter critical of the plaintiff's plans for hepatitis research on chimpanzees in West Africa. The court read *Milkovich* as establishing a rule that "except for special situations of loose, figurative, hyperbolic language, statements that contain or imply assertions of provably false fact will likely be actionable." 77 N.Y.2d at 245, 567 N.E.2d at 1275. On this test, the court believed it could be found that the letter did contain statements of fact. The court ruled, however, that under New York law, the "full context" of the statement should be taken into account, and that the letter as a whole

> would not have been viewed by the average reader of the Journal as conveying actual facts about plaintiff [and] it would be plain to the reasonable reader of this scientific publication that [the letter writer] was voicing no more than a highly partisan point of view.

77 N.Y.2d at 245, 567 N.E.2d at 1281.

One important factor to the court was that the defamation appeared in a letter to the editor.

> The public forum function of letters to the editor is closely related in spirit to the "marketplace of ideas" and oversight and informational values

that compelled recognition of the privileges of fair comment, fair report and the immunity accorded expression of opinion. These values are best effectuated by according defendant some latitude to publish a letter to the editor on a matter of legitimate public concern—the letter's author, affiliation, bias and premises fully disclosed, rebuttal openly invited—free of defamation litigation. A publication that provides a forum for such statements on controversial matters is not acting in a fashion "at odds with the premises of democratic government and with the orderly manner in which economic, social, or political change is to be effected" (Garrison v. Louisiana, 379 U.S. 64, 75, [85 S. Ct. 209, 216, 13 L. Ed. 2d 125 (1964)]), but to the contrary is fostering those very values.

Id., 567 N.E.2d at 1281-1282.

Page 1099.   After Problem 46, add the following new section:

C.   Legislative Reform of the Law of Defamation

Recent years have seen growing dissatisfaction with the way in which the law of defamation, including the constitutional rules, strikes the balance between the interest in reputation and the interest in free speech. As one critic of the defamation scene observed:

> The present law of libel is a failure. It denies most defamation victims any remedy, and at the same time chills speech by encouraging high litigation costs and occasional large judgments.[7]

Objections of this sort are not new. But as yet, legislatures have not attempted broad intervention into defamation law, as they have with respect to personal injury law—no doubt because constitutional law substantially circumscribes the permitted scope of legislative action.

Nonetheless, a movement has emerged for legislative reformation of the law of defamation—a reformation that is much more sweeping than the recent legislative reforms of tort law. The movement began with the Libel Reform Project of the Annenberg Washington Program. Under the direction of Professor Rodney A. Smolla, the project developed its comprehensive "Proposal for the Reform of Libel Law" in 1988. The basic thrust of the proposal is to provide an alternative to damage actions in which the truth or falsity of the statement would be determinative. That

---

7. Anderson, Is Libel Law Worth Reforming?, 140 U. Pa. L. Rev. 487, 550 (1991). Professor Anderson answered his question in the affirmative.

facet of the proposal has emerged in the discussion draft of the Uniform
Defamation Act of the National Conference of Commissioners on Uniform State Laws, dated December 6, 1991 (although there are significant
differences between the two). The more important features of the Uniform
Act are reprinted below.

Uniform Defamation Act

Section 1. Definitions.

In this [Act]
    (1) "Defamation" means a statement tending to harm reputation.
    (2) "Pecuniary damage" means provable economic loss. . . .

Section 2. Elements of Claim.

A person who causes the publication of a false and defamatory factual
statement about another person which harms that person's reputation is
subject to liability to that person in an action under this [Act]. Factual
statement means a communication that is reasonably understood by recipients to be of a factual nature and is objectively provable or disprov-
able.

Section 3. Burden of Proof.

In an action under this [Act]:
    (1) The plaintiff bears the burden of proving by a preponderance
of the evidence:
        (i) publication;
        (ii) defamation;
        (iii) harm to reputation; and
        (iv) falsity.
    (2) The plaintiff bears the burden of proving by clear and con-
vincing evidence:
        (i) abuse of privilege;
        (ii) negligence; and
        (iii) knowledge of falsity or reckless disregard for truth.
    (3) The plaintiff bears the burden of proving the amount of dam-
ages with reasonable certainty.

(4) The defendant bears the burden of proving by a preponderance of the evidence the facts necessary to establish a privilege. . . .

Section 5.   *Action for Vindication: Required Proof; Exclusive Remedy.*

A person bringing an action under this [Act] may elect, at the time of filing a complaint [petition], to limit the action to an action for vindication. If the election is made:

(1) the plaintiff must prove the elements stated in Section 2;

(2) the publisher may not assert absence of fault or claims of conditional privilege;

(3) damages may not be awarded; and

(4) except as provided in Section 7(b), the plaintiff may not bring an action for damages for reputational or dignitary injury caused by the publication of the false statement.

Section 6.   *Action for Vindication: Termination by Defendant.*

If at any time before 90 days after service of process in an action for vindication a defendant by motion stipulates on the record that it does not assert the truth of the publication or did not intend to assert its truth at the time of publication, or both, and agrees to publish, at the plaintiff's request, a sufficient retraction, the court shall, after the required publication, dismiss the action against the defendant making the motion.

Section 7.   *Action for Vindication; Findings of Fact; Default by Defendant.*

(a) Except as provided in subsection (b), if the plaintiff prevails in an action brought pursuant to Section 5, the court shall enter judgment which shall include written findings of fact on falsity and an order requiring the defendant, at the defendant's option:

(1) to publish the findings in conformance with Section 15(b)(1); or

(2) to pay the plaintiff an amount sufficient to secure their publication in conformance with Section 15(b)(1).

(b) If the defendant makes a motion pursuant to Section 6, but fails within a reasonable time to publish a sufficient retraction at the plaintiff's request, the plaintiff may:

(1) amend the complaint to assert a claim for damages under Section 9; or

(2) introduce evidence of falsity and, upon adequate proof of falsity, the court shall enter judgment which shall include written findings of fact on falsity and order the defendant to pay an amount sufficient to secure publication of the findings in conformance with Section 15(b)(1).

Section 8.   *Attorney's Fees and Expenses in an Action for Vindication.*

(a) In an action brought under Section 5, reasonable expenses of litigation, including attorney's fees, shall be awarded:

(1) to a prevailing plaintiff upon proof that the defendant was provided sufficient grounds for retraction in the plaintiff's request for retraction, and that a timely retraction was unreasonably refused; or

(2) to a prevailing defendant upon proof that the plaintiff had no reasonable basis upon which to allege falsity.

(b) An award of expenses and attorney's fees to a prevailing party under this section may not be disproportionate to the amount incurred by the other party for its own expenses and attorney's fees, or to the reasonable value thereof.

Section 9.   *Action for Damages.*

(a) A plaintiff may recover damages in an action under this Act if the plaintiff proves the elements of a cause of action stated in Section 2 and also proves:

(1) in a case involving conditional privilege, that the defendant published a statement with knowledge of its falsity or reckless disregard for its truth, or

(2) in all other cases, that the defendant knew or reasonably should have known the publication was false.

(b) A plaintiff entitled to recover damages under subsection (a) may recover:

(1) damages for harm to reputation and resulting emotional distress; and

(2) pecuniary damages caused by the publication.

Section 10.   Punitive Damages.

[The Act sets out alternative versions of Section 10: one would prohibit the awarding of punitive damages, and the other would permit such an award "only upon a showing by clear and convincing evidence that the defendant published the challenged statement with knowledge of its falsity and with ill will toward the plaintiff."]

*Section 11.   Attorney's Fees and Expenses in an Action for
                       Damages.*

In an action brought under Section 9, reasonable expenses of litigation, including attorney's fees, may be awarded to a prevailing plaintiff who:
    (1) made an adequate request for retraction within 60 days of publication; and
    (2) proves that the challenged statement was published with knowledge of its falsity or reckless disregard for its truth.

Section 12.   Offer of Termination in an Action for Damages.

    (a) Any time before trial of an action for damages under this [Act] a defendant, by motion, may make a termination offer. In the motion the defendant shall stipulate on the record that the defendant does not assert the truth of the publication or did not intend to assert its truth at the time of publication, or both, and the defendant shall agree:
    (1) to pay the plaintiff's reasonable expenses of litigation, including attorney's fees, incurred prior to the filing of the motion; and
    (2) to publish, at the plaintiff's request, a sufficient retraction.
    (b) If the plaintiff accepts the offer, the court shall dismiss the action against the defendant after the defendant fully complies with its terms. A plaintiff who does not accept the termination offer is limited to pecuniary damages and may not recover from the defendant making the offer the expenses of litigation, including attorney's fees.

Section 13.   Request for Retraction.

    (a) To be adequate, a request for retraction must:
    (1) be made in writing and signed by the requester or by the requester's authorized agent;

(2) identify with particularity the publication and the specific statements alleged to be false and defamatory;

(3) state the alleged defamatory meaning and identify the specific circumstances giving rise to it if the defamatory meaning arises from an implication of the publication rather than or in addition to its ordinary meaning, or from innuendo, sarcasm, or conduct; and

(4) state the alleged defamatory meaning is false.

(b) If an adequate request has not previously been made, service of [a summons and complaint [petition]] . . . constitutes an adequate request for retraction and the time for filing a responsive pleading is suspended during the period provided in Section 15 for responding to the request.

Section 14.   Effect of Retraction.

If a timely and sufficient retraction is published, a person may not bring an action for vindication based on the challenged publication under Section 5, and a person who brings an action for damages under Section 9 may recover damages only for pecuniary loss caused before the date of the retraction.

Section 15.   Timely and Sufficient Retraction.

(a) A retraction is timely if it is published before or within 30 days after receipt of a request pursuant to Section 13.

(b) A retraction is sufficient if it:

(1) is communicated in writing to the requester, is published in a manner and medium reasonably calculated to reach substantially the same audience as the publication complained of, and, if the retraction is published in another medium to conform to the 30-day period required by subsection (a), is also published in the next practicable issue or edition, if any, of the original publication; and

(2) refers to the challenged statement and:

(i) corrects the challenged statement;

(ii) in the case of a statement implied by a publication, or arising from innuendo, sarcasm, or accompanying conduct, disclaims any intent to communicate or to have communicated the implied meaning or to assert its truth; or

(iii) in the case of a statement attributed to another person, identifies that person and disclaims any intent to assert or to have asserted the truth of the statement.

(c) Notwithstanding subsection (b), a retraction is sufficient if the plaintiff states in writing that it is sufficient.

Section 16.   Absolute Privileges.

An action may not be maintained under this [Act] based on:
>   (1) a statement made:
>>   (i) in and pertaining to a judicial proceeding by a judge, attorney, witness, juror, or other participant;
>>   (ii) in and pertaining to a legislative proceeding by a legislator, attorney, aide, witness, or other participant; or
>>   (iii) in and pertaining to any quasi-judicial or quasi-legislative executive or administrative proceeding by an executive or administrative official, attorney, witness, or other participant;
>   (2) a statement that constitutes a fair and accurate report of an official action or proceeding of a governmental body, including an order or opinion of a court, or of a meeting of a governmental body which is open to the public;
>   (3) a statement published with the consent of the person harmed;
>   (4) a statement communicated between husband and wife; or
>   (5) a statement required by law to be published.

Section 17.   Conditional Privileges.

(a) A person may not be held liable for damages based on a statement that is:
>   (1) reasonably necessary to protect the publisher's legitimate interests;
>   (2) reasonably necessary to protect the legitimate interests of others;
>   (3) reasonably necessary to protect or foster a common interest between the publisher and the recipient of the communication; or
>   (4) made to a person officially charged with the duty of acting in the public interest and in relation to that person's official responsibilities.

(b) The privileges under subsection (a) are not available if the plaintiff proves that the publisher:
>   (1) unreasonably published the statement to persons other than those to whom publication was necessary to serve the interests giving rise to the privilege; or
>   (2) published the statement with knowledge of its falsity or reckless disregard for its truth.

Section 18.   Conditional Privilege for Statement Concerning Public Officials and Public Figures.

A person may not be held liable for damages based on a statement about a public official or a public figure unless the plaintiff proves that the statement was:

(1) unrelated to the person's status as a public official or public figure; or

(2) made with knowledge of its falsity or reckless disregard for its truth.

Section 19.   Liability of Republisher.

A person who republishes a statement is subject to liability under this [Act] as if the person were an original publisher.

Section 20.   Liability for Republication by Another.

A publisher is subject to liability for harm caused by a reasonably foreseeable republication by another person unless:

(1) the publisher made a sufficient retraction prior to the republication;

(2) the publisher did not publish with knowledge of falsity or reckless disregard for truth, and requested the republisher, before republication, not to publish; or

(3) the republication was made or caused by the party harmed.

Section 21.   Information Retrieval Services.

A library, archive, or similar information retrieval or transmission service providing directly or through electronic or other means access to information originally published by others is not subject to liability under Section 19 or 20 if the library, archive, or similar information retrieval or transmission service:

(1) is not reasonably understood to assert in the normal course of its business the truthfulness or reliability of the information maintained or transmitted; or

(2) takes reasonable steps to inform users that it does not assert the truthfulness or reliability of the information maintained or transmitted.

151

Chapter 13

Invasion of Privacy

> **Page 1138.** *After carryover paragraph, add the following new case:*

The Florida Star v. B.J.F.
491 U.S. 524, 109 S. Ct. 2603, 105 L. Ed. 2d 443 (1989)

Justice MARSHALL delivered the opinion of the Court.

Florida Stat. §794.03 (1987) makes it unlawful to "print, publish, or broadcast . . . in any instrument of mass communication" the name of the victim of a sexual offense.[3] Pursuant to this statute, appellant The Florida Star was found civilly liable for publishing the name of a rape victim which it had obtained from a publicly released police report. The issue presented here is whether this result comports with the First Amendment. We hold that it does not.

I

The Florida Star is a weekly newspaper which serves the community of Jacksonville, Florida, and which has an average circulation of approximately 18,000 copies. A regular feature of the newspaper is its "Police Reports" section. That section, typically two to three pages in length, contains brief articles describing local criminal incidents under police investigation.

---

3. The statute provides in its entirety:

   Unlawful to publish or broadcast information identifying sexual offense victim.— No person shall print, publish, or broadcast, or cause or allow to be printed, published, or broadcast, in any instrument of mass communication the name, address, or other identifying fact or information of the victim of any sexual offense within this chapter. An offense under this section shall constitute a misdemeanor of the second degree, punishable as provided in §775.082, §775.083, or §775.084.

Fla. Stat. §794.03 (1987).

On October 20, 1983, appellee B.J.F.[4] reported to the Duval County, Florida, Sheriff's Department (the Department) that she had been robbed and sexually assaulted by an unknown assailant. The Department prepared a report on the incident which identified B.J.F. by her full name. The Department then placed the report in its pressroom. The Department does not restrict access either to the pressroom or to the reports made available therein.

A Florida Star reporter-trainee sent to the pressroom copied the police report verbatim, including B.J.F.'s full name, on a blank duplicate of the Department's forms. A Florida Star reporter then prepared a one-paragraph article about the crime, derived entirely from the trainee's copy of the police report. The article included B.J.F.'s full name. It appeared in the "Robberies" subsection of the "Police Reports" section on October 29, 1983, one of fifty-four police blotter stories in that day's edition. The article read:

> [B.J.F.] reported on Thursday, October 20, she was crossing Brentwood Park, which is in the 500 block of Golfair Boulevard, en route to her bus stop, when an unknown black man ran up behind the lady and placed a knife to her neck and told her not to yell. The suspect then undressed the lady and had sexual intercourse with her before fleeing the scene with her 60 cents, Timex watch and gold necklace. Patrol efforts have been suspended concerning this incident because of a lack of evidence.

In printing B.J.F.'s full name, The Florida Star violated its internal policy of not publishing the names of sexual offense victims.

On September 26, 1984, B.J.F. filed suit in the Circuit Court of Duval County against the Department and The Florida Star, alleging that these parties negligently violated §794.03. Before trial, the Department settled with B.J.F. for $2,500. The Florida Star moved to dismiss, claiming, *inter alia,* that imposing civil sanctions on the newspaper pursuant to §794.03 violated the First Amendment. The trial judge rejected the motion. At the ensuing day-long trial, B.J.F. testified that she had suffered emotional distress from the publication of her name. She stated that she had heard about the article from fellow workers and acquaintances; that her mother had received several threatening phone calls from a man who stated that he would rape B.J.F. again; and that these events had forced B.J.F. to change her phone number and residence, to seek police protection, and

---

4. In filing this lawsuit, appellee used her full name in the caption of the case. On appeal, the Florida District Court of Appeal sua sponte revised the caption, stating that it would refer to the appellee by her initials, "in order to preserve [her] privacy interests." 499 So. 2d 883, 883, n. (1986). Respecting those interests, we, too, refer to appellee by her initials, both in the caption and in our discussion.

to obtain mental health counseling. In defense, The Florida Star put forth evidence indicating that the newspaper had learned B.J.F.'s name from the incident report released by the Department, and that the newspaper's violation of its internal rule against publishing the names of sexual offense victims was inadvertent.

At the close of B.J.F.'s case, and again at the close of its defense, The Florida Star moved for a directed verdict. On both occasions, the trial judge denied these motions. He ruled from the bench that §794.03 was constitutional because it reflected a proper balance between the First Amendment and privacy rights, as it applied only to a narrow set of "rather sensitive . . . criminal offenses." At the close of the newspaper's defense, the judge granted B.J.F.'s motion for a directed verdict on the issue of negligence, finding the newspaper per se negligent based upon its violation of §794.03. This ruling left the jury to consider only the questions of causation and damages. The judge instructed the jury that it could award B.J.F. punitive damages if it found that the newspaper had "acted with reckless indifference to the rights of others." The jury awarded B.J.F. $75,000 in compensatory damages and $25,000 in punitive damages. Against the actual damages award, the judge set off B.J.F.'s settlement with the Department.

The First District Court of Appeal affirmed in a three-paragraph per curiam opinion. 499 So. 2d 883 (1986). In the paragraph devoted to The Florida Star's First Amendment claim, the court stated that the directed verdict for B.J.F. had been properly entered because, under §794.03, a rape victim's name is "of a private nature and not to be published as a matter of law." Id., at 884, citing Doe v. Sarasota-Bradenton Florida Television Co., 436 So. 2d 328, 330 (Fla. App. 1983) (footnote omitted).[5] The Supreme Court of Florida denied discretionary review.

The Florida Star appealed to this Court.

II

The tension between the right which the First Amendment accords to a free press, on the one hand, and the protections which various statutes

---

5. In Doe v. Sarasota-Bradenton Florida Television Co., 436 So. 2d, at 329, the Second District Court of Appeal upheld the dismissal on First Amendment grounds of a rape victim's damage claim against a Florida television station which had broadcast portions of her testimony at her assailant's trial. The court reasoned that, as in Cox Broadcasting Corp. v. Cohn, 420 U.S. 469, 95 S. Ct. 1029, 43 L. Ed. 2d 328 (1975), the information in question "was readily available to the public, through the vehicle of a public trial." 436 So. 2d, at 330. The court stated, however, that §794.03 could constitutionally be applied to punish publication of a sexual offense victim's name or other identifying information where it had not yet become "part of an open public record" by virtue of being revealed in "open, public judicial proceedings." Ibid.

and common-law doctrines accord to personal privacy against the publication of truthful information, on the other, is a subject we have addressed several times in recent years. Our decisions in cases involving government attempts to sanction the accurate dissemination of information as invasive of privacy, have not, however, exhaustively considered this conflict. On the contrary, although our decisions have without exception upheld the press' right to publish, we have emphasized each time that we were resolving this conflict only as it arose in a discrete factual context.

The parties to this case frame their contentions in light of a trilogy of cases which have presented, in different contexts, the conflict between truthful reporting and state-protected privacy interests. In Cox Broadcasting Corp. v. Cohn, 420 U.S. 469, 95 S. Ct. 1029, 43 L. Ed. 2d 328 (1975), we found unconstitutional a civil damages award entered against a television station for broadcasting the name of a rape-murder victim which the station had obtained from courthouse records. In Oklahoma Publishing Co. v. Oklahoma County District Court, 430 U.S. 308, 97 S. Ct. 1045, 51 L. Ed. 2d 355 (1977), we found unconstitutional a state court's pretrial order enjoining the media from publishing the name or photograph of an 11-year-old boy in connection with a juvenile proceeding involving that child which reporters had attended. Finally, in Smith v. Daily Mail Publishing Co., 443 U.S. 97, 99 S. Ct. 2667, 61 L. Ed. 2d 399 (1979), we found unconstitutional the indictment of two newspapers for violating a state statute forbidding newspapers to publish, without written approval of the juvenile court, the name of any youth charged as a juvenile offender. The papers had learned about a shooting by monitoring a police band radio frequency and had obtained the name of the alleged juvenile assailant from witnesses, the police, and a local prosecutor.

Appellant takes the position that this case is indistinguishable from *Cox Broadcasting*. Alternatively, it urges that our decisions in the above trilogy, and in other cases in which we have held that the right of the press to publish truth overcame asserted interests other than personal privacy, can be distilled to yield a broader First Amendment principle that the press may never be punished, civilly or criminally, for publishing the truth. Appellee counters that the privacy trilogy is inapposite, because in each case the private information already appeared on a "public record," and because the privacy interests at stake were far less profound than in the present case. In the alternative, appellee urges that *Cox Broadcasting* be overruled and replaced with a categorical rule that publication of the name of a rape victim never enjoys constitutional protection.

We conclude that imposing damages on appellant for publishing B.J.F.'s name violates the First Amendment, although not for either of the reasons appellant urges. Despite the strong resemblance this case bears to *Cox*

Broadcasting, that case cannot fairly be read as controlling here. The name of the rape victim in that case was obtained from courthouse records that were open to public inspection, a fact which Justice White's opinion for the Court repeatedly noted. . . . Significantly, one of the reasons we gave in *Cox Broadcasting* for invalidating the challenged damages award was the important role the press plays in subjecting trials to public scrutiny and thereby helping guarantee their fairness. That role is not directly compromised where, as here, the information in question comes from a police report prepared and disseminated at a time at which not only had no adversarial criminal proceedings begun, but no suspect had been identified.

Nor need we accept appellant's invitation to hold broadly that truthful publication may never be punished consistent with the First Amendment. Our cases have carefully eschewed reaching this ultimate question, mindful that the future may bring scenarios which prudence counsels our not resolving anticipatorily. See, e.g., Near v. Minnesota ex rel. Olson, 283 U.S. 697, 716, 51 S. Ct. 625, 75 L. Ed. 1357 (1931) (hypothesizing "publication of the sailing dates of transports or the number and location of troops"); see also Garrison v. Louisiana, 379 U.S. 64, 72, n.8, 74, 85 S. Ct. 209, 215, n.8, 216, 13 L. Ed. 2d 125 (1964) (endorsing absolute defense of truth "where discussion of public affairs is concerned," but leaving unsettled the constitutional implications of truthfulness "in the discrete area of purely private libels"). . . . We continue to believe that the sensitivity and significance of the interests presented in clashes between First Amendment and privacy rights counsel relying on limited principles that sweep no more broadly than the appropriate context of the instant case.

In our view, this case is appropriately analyzed with reference to such a limited First Amendment principle. It is the one, in fact, which we articulated in *Daily Mail* in our synthesis of prior cases involving attempts to punish truthful publication: "[I]f a newspaper lawfully obtains truthful information about a matter of public significance then state officials may not constitutionally punish publication of the information, absent a need to further a state interest of the highest order." 443 U.S., at 103, 99 S. Ct., at 2671. . . .

. . . Appellee argues that a rule punishing publication furthers three closely related interests: the privacy of victims of sexual offenses; the physical safety of such victims, who may be targeted for retaliation if their names become known to their assailants; and the goal of encouraging victims of such crimes to report these offenses without fear of exposure.

At a time in which we are daily reminded of the tragic reality of rape, it is undeniable that these are highly significant interests, a fact underscored by the Florida Legislature's explicit attempt to protect these interests by enacting a criminal statute prohibiting much dissemination of victim identities. We accordingly do not rule out the possibility that, in a proper case, imposing civil sanctions for publication of the name of a rape victim might be so overwhelmingly necessary to advance these interests as to satisfy the *Daily Mail* standard. For three independent reasons, however, imposing liability for publication under the circumstances of this case is too precipitous a means of advancing these interests to convince us that there is a "need" within the meaning of the *Daily Mail* formulation for Florida to take this extreme step. Cf. Landmark Communications, [Inc. v. Virginia, 435 U.S. 829, 98 S. Ct. 1535, 56 L. Ed. 2d 1 (1978)] (invalidating penalty on publication despite State's expressed interest in nondissemination, reflected in statute prohibiting unauthorized divulging of names of judges under investigation).

First is the manner in which appellant obtained the identifying information in question. As we have noted, where the government itself provides information to the media, it is most appropriate to assume that the government had, but failed to utilize, far more limited means of guarding against dissemination than the extreme step of punishing truthful speech. That assumption is richly borne out in this case. B.J.F.'s identity would never have come to light were it not for the erroneous, if inadvertent, inclusion by the Department of her full name in an incident report made available in a pressroom open to the public. . . .

That appellant gained access to the information in question through a government news release makes it especially likely that, if liability were to be imposed, self-censorship would result. Reliance on a news release is a paradigmatically "routine newspaper reporting techniqu[e]." *Daily Mail,* 443 U.S., at 103, 99 S. Ct., at 2671. The government's issuance of such a release, without qualification, can only convey to recipients that the government considered dissemination lawful, and indeed expected the recipients to disseminate the information further. Had appellant merely reproduced the news release prepared and released by the Department, imposing civil damages would surely violate the First Amendment. The fact that appellant converted the police report into a news story by adding the linguistic connecting tissue necessary to transform the report's facts into full sentences cannot change this result.

A second problem with Florida's imposition of liability for publication is the broad sweep of the negligence per se standard applied under the civil cause of action implied from §794.03. Unlike claims based on the common law tort of invasion of privacy, see Restatement (Second) of Torts §652D (1977), civil actions based on §794.03 require no case-by-case findings that the disclosure of a fact about a person's private life was one that a reasonable person would find highly offensive. On the contrary, under the per se theory of negligence adopted by the courts below, liability follows automatically from publication. This is so regardless of whether the identity of the victim is already known throughout the community; whether the victim has voluntarily called public attention to the offense; or whether the identity of the victim has otherwise become a reasonable subject of public concern—because, perhaps, questions have arisen whether the victim fabricated an assault by a particular person. Nor is there a scienter requirement of any kind under §794.03, engendering the perverse result that truthful publications challenged pursuant to this cause of action are less protected by the First Amendment than even the least protected defamatory falsehoods: those involving purely private figures, where liability is evaluated under a standard, usually applied by a jury, of ordinary negligence. . . .

Third, and finally, the facial underinclusiveness of §794.03 raises serious doubts about whether Florida is, in fact, serving, with this statute, the significant interests which appellee invokes in support of affirmance. Section 794.03 prohibits the publication of identifying information only if this information appears in an "instrument of mass communication," a term the statute does not define. Section 794.03 does not prohibit the spread by other means of the identities of victims of sexual offenses. An individual who maliciously spreads word of the identity of a rape victim is thus not covered, despite the fact that the communication of such information to persons who live near, or work with, the victim may have consequences as devastating as the exposure of her name to large numbers of strangers. . . .

When a State attempts the extraordinary measure of punishing truthful publication in the name of privacy, it must demonstrate its commitment to advancing this interest by applying its prohibition evenhandedly, to the small-time disseminator as well as the media giant. Where important First Amendment interests are at stake, the mass scope of disclosure is not an acceptable surrogate for injury. A ban on disclosures effected by "instrument[s] of mass communication" simply cannot be defended on the ground that partial prohibitions may effect partial relief. . . .

III

Our holding today is limited. We do not hold that truthful publication is automatically constitutionally protected, or that there is no zone of personal privacy within which the State may protect the individual from intrusion by the press, or even that a State may never punish publication of the name of a victim of a sexual offense. We hold only that where a newspaper publishes truthful information which it has lawfully obtained, punishment may lawfully be imposed, if at all, only when narrowly tailored to a state interest of the highest order, and that no such interest is satisfactorily served by imposing liability under §794.03 to appellant under the facts of this case. The decision below is therefore

Reversed.

Justice SCALIA, concurring in part and concurring in the judgment.

I think it sufficient to decide this case to rely upon the third ground set forth in the Court's opinion, ante, at 15-16: that a law cannot be regarded as protecting an interest "of the highest order," Smith v. Daily Mail Publishing Co., 443 U.S. 97, 103, 99 S. Ct. 2667, 2670-71, 61 L. Ed. 2d 399 (1979), and thus as justifying a restriction upon truthful speech, when it leaves appreciable damage to that supposedly vital interest unprohibited. In the present case, I would anticipate that the rape victim's discomfort at the dissemination of news of her misfortune among friends and acquaintances would be at least as great as her discomfort at its publication by the media to people to whom she is only a name. Yet the law in question does not prohibit the former in either oral or written form. Nor is it at all clear, as I think it must be to validate this statute, that Florida's general privacy law would prohibit such gossip. Nor, finally, is it credible that the interest meant to be served by the statute is the protection of the victim against a rapist still at large—an interest that arguably would extend only to mass publication. . . .

This law has every appearance of a prohibition that society is prepared to impose upon the press but not upon itself. Such a prohibition does not protect an interest "of the highest order." For that reason, I agree that the judgment of the court below must be reversed.

Justice WHITE, with whom THE CHIEF JUSTICE and Justice O'CONNOR join, dissenting.

"Short of homicide, [rape] is the 'ultimate violation of self.' " Coker v. Georgia, 433 U.S. 584, 597, 97 S. Ct. 2861, 2869, 53 L. Ed. 2d 982 (1977) (opinion of White, J.). For B.J.F., however, the violation she suffered at a rapist's knife-point marked only the beginning of her ordeal. A week later, while her assailant was still at large, an account of this assault—identifying by name B.J.F. as the victim—was published by The Florida Star. As a result, B.J.F. received harassing phone calls, required mental health counseling, was forced to move from her home, and was even threatened with being raped again.

Yet today, the Court holds that a jury award of $75,000 to compensate B.J.F. for the harm she suffered due to the Star's negligence is at odds with the First Amendment. I do not accept this result.

The Court reaches its conclusion based on an analysis of three of our precedents and a concern with three particular aspects of the judgment against appellant. I consider each of these points in turn, and then consider some of the larger issues implicated by today's decision.

I

The Court finds its result compelled, or at least supported in varying degrees, by three of our prior cases: Cox Broadcasting Corp. v. Cohn, 420 U.S. 469, 95 S. Ct. 1029, 43 L. Ed. 2d 328 (1975); Oklahoma Publishing Co. v. Oklahoma County District Court, 430 U.S. 308, 97 S. Ct. 1045, 51 L. Ed. 2d 355 (1977); and Smith v. Daily Mail Publishing Co., 443 U.S. 97, 99 S. Ct. 2667, 61 L. Ed. 2d 399 (1979). I disagree. None of these cases requires the harsh outcome reached today.

Cox Broadcasting reversed a damages award entered against a television station, which had obtained a rape victim's name from public records maintained in connection with the judicial proceedings brought against her assailants. While there are similarities, critical aspects of that case make it wholly distinguishable from this one. First, in *Cox Broadcasting*, the victim's name had been disclosed in the hearing where her assailants pleaded guilty; and, as we recognized, judicial records have always been considered public information in this country. . . . In fact, even the earliest notion of privacy rights exempted the information contained in judicial records from its protections. See Warren & Brandeis, The Right to Privacy, 4 Harv. L. Rev. 193, 216-217 (1890). Second, unlike the incident report at issue here, which was meant by state law to be withheld from public release, the judicial proceedings at issue in *Cox Broadcasting* were open as a matter of state law. Thus, in *Cox Broadcasting*, the state-law scheme made public disclosure of the victim's name almost inevitable; here, Florida law forbids such disclosure. See Fla. Stat. §794.03 (1987).

These facts—that the disclosure came in judicial proceedings, which were open to the public—were critical to our analysis in *Cox Broadcasting*. The distinction between that case and this one is made obvious by the penultimate paragraph of *Cox Broadcasting*:

> We are reluctant to embark on a course that would make *public records generally available to the media* but would forbid their publication if offensive. . . . [T]he First and Fourteenth Amendments will not allow exposing the press to liability for truthfully publishing information *released to the public in official court records. If there are privacy interests to be protected in judicial proceedings, the States must respond by means which avoid public documentation or other exposure of private information.* . . . Once true information is disclosed in *public court documents open to public inspection,* the press cannot be sanctioned for publishing it.

Cox Broadcasting, supra, at 496, 95 S. Ct., at 1047 (emphasis added).

Cox Broadcasting stands for the proposition that the State cannot make the press its first line of defense in withholding private information from the public—it cannot ask the press to secrete private facts that the State makes no effort to safeguard in the first place. In this case, however, the State has undertaken "means which avoid [but obviously, not altogether prevent] public documentation or other exposure of private information." No doubt this is why the Court frankly admits that "*Cox Broadcasting* . . . cannot fairly be read as controlling here." . . .

II

We are left, then, to wonder whether the three "independent reasons" the Court cites for reversing the judgment for B.J.F. support its result.

The first of these reasons relied on by the Court is the fact "appellant gained access to [B.J.F.'s name] through a government news release." "The government's issuance of such a release, without qualification, can only convey to recipients that the government considered dissemination lawful," the Court suggests. So described, this case begins to look like the situation in *Oklahoma Publishing,* where a judge invited reporters into his courtroom, but then tried to forbid them from reporting on the proceedings they observed. But this case is profoundly different. Here, the "release" of information provided by the government was not, as the Court says, "without qualification." As the Star's own reporter conceded at trial, the crime incident report that inadvertently included B.J.F.'s name was posted in a room that contained signs making it clear that the names of rape victims were not matters of public record, and were not to be published. The Star's reporter indicated that she understood that she "[was not] allowed to take down that information" (i.e., B.J.F.'s name) and that she "[was] not supposed to take the information from the police department." Thus, by her own admission the posting of the incident report did not convey to the Star's reporter the idea that "the government considered dissemination lawful"; the Court's suggestion to the contrary is inapt.

Instead, Florida has done precisely what we suggested, in *Cox Broadcasting,* that States wishing to protect the privacy rights of rape victims might do: "respond [to the challenge] by means which *avoid* public documentation or other exposure of private information." 420 U.S., at 496, 95 S. Ct., at 1047 (emphasis added). By amending its public records statute to exempt rape victims' names from disclosure, Fla. Stat. §119.07(3)(h) (1983), and forbidding its officials from releasing such information, Fla. Stat. §794.03 (1983), the State has taken virtually every step imaginable to prevent what happened here. This case presents a far cry, then, from *Cox Broadcasting* or *Oklahoma Publishing,* where the State asked the news media not to publish information it had made generally available to the public: here, the State is not asking the media to do the State's job in the first instance.

Unfortunately, as this case illustrates, mistakes happen: even when States take measures to "avoid" disclosure, sometimes rape victims' names are found out. As I see it, it is not too much to ask the press, in instances such as this, to respect simple standards of decency and refrain from publishing a victims' name, address, and/or phone number.[6]

Second, the Court complains that appellant was judged here under too strict a liability standard. The Court contends that a newspaper might be found liable under the Florida courts' negligence per se theory without regard to a newspaper's scienter or degree of fault. Ante, at 2612. The short answer to this complaint is that whatever merit the Court's argument might have, it is wholly inapposite here, where the jury found that appellant acted with "reckless indifference towards the rights of others," 2 Record 170, a standard far higher than the *Gertz* standard [Gertz v. Robert Welch, Inc., 418 U.S. 323, 94 S. Ct. 2997, 41 L. Ed. 2d 789 (1974)] the Court urges as a constitutional minimum today. Ante, at 2612. B.J.F. proved the Star's negligence at trial—and, actually, far more than simple negligence; the Court's concerns about damages resting on a strict liability or mere causation basis are irrelevant to the validity of the judgment for appellee.

But even taking the Court's concerns in the abstract, they miss the mark. Permitting liability under a negligence per se theory does not mean that defendants will be held liable without a showing of negligence, but rather, that the standard of care has been set by the legislature, instead of the courts. The Court says that negligence per se permits a plaintiff to

---

6. The Court's concern for a free press is appropriate, but such concerns should be balanced against rival interests in a civilized and humane society. An absolutist view of the former leads to insensitivity as to the latter.

This was evidenced at trial, when the Florida Star's lawyer explained why the paper was not to blame for any anguish caused B.J.F. by a phone call she received, the day after the Star's story was published, from a man threatening to rape B.J.F. again. Noting that the phone call was received at B.J.F.'s home by her mother (who was babysitting B.J.F.'s children while B.J.F. was in the hospital), who relayed the threat to B.J.F., the Star's counsel suggested:

> [I]n reference to the [threatening] phone call, it is sort of blunted by the fact that [B.J.F.] didn't receive the phone call. Her mother did. And if there is any pain and suffering in connection with the phone call, it has to lay in her mother's hands. I mean, my God, she called [B.J.F.] up at the hospital to tell her [of the threat]—you know, I think that is tragic, but I don't think that is something you can blame the Florida Star for.

2 Record 154-155.

While I would not want to live in a society where freedom of the press was unduly limited, I also find regrettable an interpretation of the First Amendment that fosters such a degree of irresponsibility on the part of the news media.

hold a defendant liable without a showing that the disclosure was "of a fact about a person's private life . . . that a reasonable person would find highly offensive." Ibid. But the point here is that the legislature—reflecting popular sentiment—has determined that disclosure of the fact that a person was raped is categorically a revelation that reasonable people find offensive. And as for the Court's suggestion that the Florida courts' theory permits liability without regard for whether the victim's identity is already known, or whether she herself has made it known—these are facts that would surely enter into the calculation of damages in such a case. In any event, none of these mitigating factors was present here; whatever the force of these arguments generally, they do not justify the Court's ruling against B.J.F. in this case.

Third, the Court faults the Florida criminal statute for being underinclusive: §794.03 covers disclosure of rape victims' names in " 'instrument[s] of mass communication,' " but not other means of distribution, the Court observes. Ante, at 2612-2613. But our cases which have struck down laws that limit or burden the press due to their underinclusiveness have involved situations where a legislature has singled out one segment of the news media or press for adverse treatment, see, e.g., *Daily Mail* (restricting newspapers and not radio or television), or singled out the press for adverse treatment when compared to other similarly situated enterprises, see, e.g., Minneapolis Star & Tribune Co. v. Minnesota Commr. of Revenue, 460 U.S. 575, 578, 103 S. Ct. 1365, 1368, 75 L. Ed. 2d 295 (1983). Here, the Florida law evenhandedly covers all "instrument[s] of mass communication" no matter their form, media, content, nature, or purpose. It excludes neighborhood gossips because presumably the Florida Legislature has determined that neighborhood gossips do not pose the danger and intrusion to rape victims that "instrument[s] of mass communication" do. Simply put: Florida wanted to prevent the widespread distribution of rape victims' names, and therefore enacted a statute tailored almost as precisely as possible to achieving that end. . . .

Consequently, neither the State's "dissemination" of B.J.F.'s name, nor the standard of liability imposed here, nor the underinclusiveness of Florida tort law requires setting aside the verdict for B.J.F. . . .

III . . .

Of course, the right to privacy is not absolute. Even the article widely relied upon in cases vindicating privacy rights, Warren & Brandeis, The Right to Privacy, 4 Harv. L. Rev. 193 (1890), recognized that this right inevitably conflicts with the public's right to know about matters of general concern—and that sometimes, the latter must trump the former. Resolving this conflict is a difficult matter, and I fault the Court not for attempting to strike an appropriate balance between the two, but rather, fault it for according too little weight to B.J.F.'s side of [the] equation, and too much on the other.

I would strike the balance rather differently. Writing for the Ninth Circuit, Judge Merrill put this view eloquently:

> Does the spirit of the Bill of Rights require that individuals be free to pry into the unnewsworthy private affairs of their fellowmen? In our view it does not. In our view, fairly defined areas of privacy must have the protection of law if the quality of life is to continue to be reasonably acceptable. The public's right to know is, then, subject to reasonable limitations so far as concerns the private facts of its individual members.

Virgil v. Time, Inc., 527 F.2d 1122, 1128 (1975), *cert. denied,* 425 U.S. 998, 96 S. Ct. 2215, 48 L. Ed. 2d 823 (1976). . . .

I do not suggest that the Court's decision today is a radical departure from a previously charted course. The Court's ruling has been foreshadowed.

In Time, Inc. v. Hill, 385 U.S. 374, 383-384, n.7, 87 S. Ct. 534, 539-540, n.7, 17 L. Ed. 2d 456 (1967), we observed that—after a brief period early in this century where Brandeis' view was ascendant—the trend in "modern" jurisprudence has been to eclipse an individual's right to maintain private any truthful information that the press wished to publish. More recently, in *Cox Broadcasting,* 420 U.S. at 491, 95 S. Ct., at 1044, we acknowledged the possibility that the First Amendment may prevent a State from ever subjecting the publication of truthful but private information to civil liability. Today, we hit the bottom of the slippery slope.

I would find a place to draw the line higher on the hillside: a spot high enough to protect B.J.F.'s desire for privacy and peace-of-mind in the wake of a horrible personal tragedy. There is no public interest in publishing the names, addresses, and phone numbers of persons who are the victims of crime—and no public interest in immunizing the press from liability in the rare cases where a State's efforts to protect a victim's privacy have failed.

Consequently, I respectfully dissent.

Chapter 14

Commercial Torts: Misrepresentation and Interference with Business Relations

B. Interference with Business Relations

2. Intentional Interference with Prospective Contracts

Page 1216. After last paragraph, add the following text:

Wrongful discharge is the subject of the Model Uniform Employment Termination Act, adopted by the National Conference of Commissioners on Uniform State Laws in August 1991. Except as otherwise permitted by the Act, an employer could not discharge an employee without "good cause." Good cause is defined as:

> (i) a reasonable basis related to an individual employee for termination of the employee's employment in view of relevant factors and circumstances, which may include the employee's duties, responsibilities, conduct (on the job or otherwise), job performance, and employment record, or (ii) the exercise of business judgment in good faith by the employer, including setting its economic or institutional goals and determining methods to achieve those goals, organizing or reorganizing operations, discontinuing, consolidating, or divesting operations or positions or parts of operations or positions, determining the size of its work force and the nature of the positions filled by its work force, and determining and changing standards of performance for positions.

The Model Act leaves room for alterations by contract between the employer and the employee of the rights otherwise given the employee by the Act. If there is an express agreement, the good cause requirement can be waived if the employer agrees to pay the employee on termination one month's pay for each year of employment. Further, the discharge for good cause requirement does not apply to the termination of employment at the end of an expressly agreed-on specified period of employment "related to the completion of a specified task, project, undertaking, or assignment."

The Model Act also establishes methods of enforcement of its provisions.